I Can Breastfeed

Photo by Elisha Rain

I Can Breastfeed

Visualize Your Way to Breastfeeding Success

. . . .

KRISTINA CHAMBERLAIN
CNM, ARNP, IBCLC

Gina,
To the best mentor
I've ever had!
Krista Chll

iUniverse, Inc.
New York   Bloomington

I Can Breastfeed
Visualize Your Way to Breastfeeding Success

iUniverse books may be ordered through booksellers or by contacting:

iUniverse
1663 Liberty Drive
Bloomington, IN 47403
www.iuniverse.com
1-800-Authors (1-800-288-4677)

ISBN: 978-1-4502-5397-0 (pbk)
ISBN: 978-1-4502-5398-7 (cloth)
ISBN: 978-1-4502-5399-4 (ebk)

Printed in the United States of America

iUniverse rev. date: 9/4/2010

Author's Photo Credit: Dorcas Caraballo

To Lucy and Ruby for teaching me more about
breastfeeding (and love) than any book ever could.

Contents

Acknowledgments

Thank you to the following people:

Mom, for exposing me to visualization and affirmation at a young age, Debi Fairman, Susan Nowers, Amy Miller, Julia Curren, Betsy Godwin, Ann-Marie Speirs, Ellen Welcker, Stephanie Wright, Sabrina Klein, Darla Benedict, Holly Nelson, Heather Bradford, Karma Tiffany, Teresa Goodwin, and Elizabeth Scarborough for sharing their stories, Doria Keesling and Cynthia Gabriel, for giving me what I needed to turn this into a book, Gwenan Wilbur and Alicia Robinson, for making me look good, and to Leon, for being my cheerleader while I was nursing our daughters

This book provides information and motivation for a successful breastfeeding experience for the whole family. It is not intended to replace the services of a lactation consultant, if needed. If you or your baby is having difficulties, pain, poor weight gain, or any other concerns, contact your lactation consultant or your health care provider for guidance.

Introduction
I've Been There Too!

· · · · · · · · · · ·

CONGRATULATIONS ON YOUR PREGNANCY! Pregnancy is a very exciting time. You will discover so many new things about your baby and yourself as this relationship develops, and breastfeeding will add another layer to your union. If you have already given birth to your baby, no doubt you have been in awe and overwhelmed with emotions ever since.

The purpose of this book is to foster a successful and satisfying breastfeeding relationship between you and your baby. My goal is to educate you on what all this breastfeeding business is about and to instill confidence. You will not only believe but *know*, without a doubt, that you and your baby can have a successful breastfeeding experience. You will be more prepared to avoid obstacles, or address those that might arise.

I know what it's like to have the romantic idea that breastfeeding is a wonderful, special event between only you and your baby. And it is...except when it's not. When your baby doesn't immediately latch, or your milk doesn't just pour, or something just isn't working, it can leave you with a feeling of disappointment, frustration, and like the world just duped you. This is a very real experience for many women, until they get help or until the light bulb goes on for themselves and their babies.

I worked with breastfeeding moms for years as a doula, nurse-midwife, and lactation consultant before I breastfed my own daughters. I was trained by a very prominent and well-respected lactation consultant at the University of Washington Medical Center. I received my midwifery degree from the best nursing school in the country. I had the knowledge and did my job well. I felt that I was really good at educating women on breastfeeding issues and thought it could always be easy if women just had support and some basic information. Imagine how utterly shocked I was to have breastfeeding problems myself when my first daughter was born. Here I was, overeducated, sleep deprived and second guessing everything I did. I talked to no less than eleven lactation consultants in the first two months of my daughter's life. I remember waking up when she was two weeks old. I was crying hysterically because I was convinced we weren't going to figure this nursing stuff out and I wouldn't be able to breastfeed. Worse, I would have to give my baby formula.

I was lucky to have a very supportive husband who was totally sold on the idea that "breast is best" and to have friends who were experienced moms who could help me take a step back and calm down. It wasn't easy, and I admit, I didn't like being a mom for the first 3 months of my oldest daughter's life. But, with lots of commitment I got over my emotional breakdown and breastfed my daughter. She gained weight, improved her suck, and we both loved nursing for 20 months. I don't mean to scare you by telling my story. I tell it to show that breastfeeding can be difficult for anyone, even "experts," and that with determination, support, and help, it can be done for as long as mom and baby desire. I can also say that having a second (or third, etc) baby can make a mama feel even more confident. I had a much better breastfeeding experience the second time around because I was more confident and prepared for what to expect. I nursed my second daughter for 2 years.

Another reason I decided to write a book about breastfeeding is that I wanted to give women a new way of looking at this topic. I have worked with many women stressed out by the idea that they don't have enough milk for their baby when, in fact, they do. They don't *trust* that their body can produce what their baby needs, and then some. They don't *believe* that their baby is getting the nourishment he needs from breast milk alone. They don't *feel confident* that the act of breastfeeding their baby will get easier and easier as both mom and baby learn how to do it. They aren't fully *committed* to giving their baby the optimal nutrition that only breast milk can provide, so they give up too easily.

Of course there are days when breast feeding can be hard, frustrating, and even painful. Those days can really suck. My worst days were during the first three weeks of my oldest daughter's life. I didn't leave the house. I didn't put on a bra. What was the point? I was nursing and pumping every two hours- so often that I usually went without a shirt! But days like that are few in number compared to the overall breastfeeding experience. Because we no longer live in communities where older women help younger women with birth, breastfeeding, childrearing, etc., we are left to doubt our own abilities. We don't see what nursing looks like from watching real women in our communities. This is why we read books and go to classes. We want this information, but have nowhere else to get it. We have turned this very natural relationship into a scientific process. I am concerned that women don't have access to the information and support needed to be successful at these things. I hope that this book can empower you and give you the information you need for success. And of course, if more hands-on help is needed, please contact a lactation consultant, postpartum nurse, midwife, or doctor.

Knowledge, Commitment, & Access

If you get nothing else out of this book, I hope you believe two things when you have finished reading it:

1) You will have enough milk to exclusively breastfeed your baby for the first 6 months, and to continue breastfeeding after that for as long as mom and baby desire.

2) Breast milk is the best thing to give your baby as a foundation for a lifetime of good health.

My experience working with pregnant and breastfeeding moms has taught me that there is a recipe to successful breastfeeding. But, before you even latch that baby on, you need to:

KNOW that you can feed your baby exclusively breast milk. Few women have "no milk". Better yet, **KNOW** that your baby will thrive on just your milk.

COMMIT to the act of breastfeeding. What you are doing has a purpose and the benefits last a lifetime.

Have **ACCESS** to support from your partner, family, and health care providers.

With these three things in place, you can overcome many obstacles. Sore nipples and sleep deprivation be damned! You will give your baby your milk!

Think about how you were fed as a baby. Unless you were breastfed as a toddler, you probably don't remember the experience. If you were breastfed, ask your mother what her memory of this was. Did she enjoy it, have an easy time, face any difficulties? How do you feel about the fact that you were breastfed? Conversely, how do you feel knowing you were not breastfed, if this is the case? Has knowing whether or not you were breastfed affected your decision to breastfeed your own baby?

Think about who supports your decision to breastfeed. Studies have shown that the most important factor in a successful breastfeeding experience is the support a mom gets from her partner and family. Is your partner as invested in your decision to breastfeed as you are? Does your partner understand that breast milk provides optimal nutrition for your baby? How does your partner feel about the idea of you breastfeeding in public? If your mother did not breastfeed her children, will she support your desire to breastfeed yours? It's important to have a team of cheerleaders supporting you when you breastfeed, especially at two in the morning when things feel harder than ever expected.

Talk about your decision to breastfeed with your family members while you are pregnant so they know how important this is to you. If they need education about the benefits of breastfeeding, by all means, educate them. There was a time, not too long ago, when breastfeeding was out of fashion in this country. Doctors pushed formula on new mothers with the belief that it was better. Now we know better. (If your health care provider is pushing formula on you, change providers!)

This book is about breastfeeding. It is not about formula feeding your baby with cow's milk. (Yes, formula is made from cow's milk.) I won't be talking much about formula. I won't even compare breast milk to formula because there is no comparison! I will offer information about formula to illustrate a point if necessary. Formula should be treated as medicine: if a baby needs to be fed, and breast milk isn't an option for some reason, formula should be given for the survival of that baby. However, if breast milk is available, formula shouldn't even be in the picture. As with most medicines, formula has helped many babies survive situations they would not have before formula was created. It is not comparable to breast milk, but it can literally be a life saver at times.

There are a couple more things you can do before your baby is born to foster success with breastfeeding, which are discussed in Chapter 3. If you are reading this book after your baby is born, you may still benefit from some of the information in this chapter, such as the selection of a postpartum doula. Or you can use the information before your next baby is born!

How This Book Is Organized

Throughout the book, you will hear real moms' thoughts on their breastfeeding experience. Some had a very easy time nursing their baby. Others had to overcome some struggles. All are happy that they breastfed their babies and experienced that relationship. Because we do not live in communities where women mentor each other in the ways of womanhood like our ancestors did, I have included their stories to give you more evidence that moms are meant to nourish their babies with their milk and to highlight how wonderful that job can be.

You will also find a visualization exercise at the end of each chapter. These exercises, along with the affirmations found though out the book and in Appendix 1, are what make this book different from the other breastfeeding books. My goal is to convince you that these tools can lead to a successful breastfeeding relationship with your baby. I will talk more about what exercises are and how to use them in Chapter 2.

Chapter 1

You Can Do It. Yes, You Can!
But Why?

• • • • • • • • • • •

My breasts know exactly how
much milk my baby needs.

BREASTFEEDING IS THE GIFT of ideal nutrition and the best start for good health. Breast milk is the *optimal* food for your baby, providing the healthiest foundation for her immune system and overall future health. Breastfeeding also allows time for you and your baby to slow down and connect with each other. Dads and partners can be confident that breastfeeding provides their baby with the best nutrition possible. The whole family benefits from breastfeeding! Breastfeeding also benefits society as a whole.

The American Academy of Pediatrics recommends exclusive breastfeeding for the first 6 months of life, and continued breastfeeding for at least the next 6 months. (1) In other words, breastfeed your baby for at least a year, even if you are feeding her solid food by then. All benefits of breastfeeding continue the longer you breastfeed. In America, about 72% of moms start breastfeeding their babies at birth. At 6 months, that rate drops to about 14%. (2) That's too low! Many moms and babies are missing out on the long-term benefits of breastfeeding. According to the Center for Disease Control (CDC), a goal of the Healthy People 2010 Initiative was for breastfeeding rates at 6 months postpartum to increase to 50%, and to 25% at one year. This would have a great positive impact on the overall health of our country, improving quality of life, decreasing chronic illness, and decreasing the amount of health care dollars spent because breastfed babies grow up to be healthier adults.

Why are so few moms still nursing at 6 months? Lack of support is

1

probably the biggest reason: lack of support from family, lack of support from employers, and lack of support from society in general, not to mention a non-supportive maternity leave in this country. As a society, we don't wholly embrace nursing our babies as normal. Children's books often show babies feeding from a bottle, rather than a breast. Women are still asked to cover up or leave public places when nursing their babies in some states. Nursing a toddler is negatively judged by many, so moms keep it a secret. Somewhere along the way (right around when formula was created and given free to new moms in the hospital), breastfeeding got a bad reputation and we have been working to change it ever since.

Components of Breast Milk

What is in breast milk? What makes it so delicious and nutritious for our babes? We probably don't know everything included in this living liquid, but here is what we do know about the composition of human milk:

Breast milk is made mostly of **water**, about 87%. It provides all of the water a baby needs, even on really hot days. (3)

Protein is synthesized from amino acids, which are the building blocks of all cells. These amino acids come from the mother's blood and are important for the development of the central nervous system. There are 2 types of proteins: casein (curd), which makes up 40% of the proteins and whey (lactalbumins), which makes up 60% of the proteins. (4) (3)

Whey proteins have infection protective properties; it inhibits the growth of certain bacteria in the baby's gut. It also protects against respiratory illness and allergies.

The casein found in human milk allows more iron to be absorbed by the baby's body. This is especially important because iron is found in low amounts in human milk.

Protein enzymes have an anti-inflammatory function and are antimicrobial. They also promote the growth of beneficial bacteria in the gut and aid in the development of intestinal tissue.

The main **carbohydrate** found in human milk is lactose. High amounts of lactose create a more acidic environment in the baby's gut, which decreases the amount of "bad" bacteria. It also improves the absorption of calcium, phosphorus, and magnesium.

Fat is a vehicle for fat soluble vitamins and cholesterol necessary for brain development and a precursor for prostaglandins and hormones. The majority of calories in human milk come from fat.

There are many **vitamins** found in human milk. The fat soluble vitamins are A, D, E, and K. The water soluble vitamins are C, thiamin, riboflavin, niacin, B6, folate, B12, biotin, and panthothenic acid. (4) (3)

The **minerals** found in human milk are phosphorus, calcium, and magnesium. (4)

The **electrolytes** found in human milk are potassium, sodium, and chloride. (4)

The **trace elements** found in human milk are zinc, iron, iodine, copper, manganese, selenium, chromium, and cobalt. (4)

There are also plenty of white blood cells (WBCs) in human milk. The job of WBCs are to fight infection: another reason breast milk is so great at keeping your baby healthy!

Benefits to Baby

Breast milk provides probiotics (good bacteria) to your baby so that her gut begins to work properly. Breast milk also contains disease-fighting antibodies. These antibodies lay the foundation for the immune system of your baby. Thus, breastfed babies are healthier and get fewer infections. When mom is sick, her body produces the antibodies to fight that particular illness. These antibodies pass through the breast milk to the baby, giving him protection from the very illness his mother has.

Babies utilize the nutrients of breast milk more efficiently, so it is digested more easily. This means that a baby fed breast milk will empty his stomach sooner than a baby fed formula. Most formula is made from cow's milk or is soy based. Cow's milk digests more slowly, sitting in the baby's gut longer, curdling. This results in more gas, colic, constipation, and spitting up.

Breast milk contains cholesterol, which is only found in very small amounts in formula. This cholesterol is thought to help adults combat high "bad" cholesterol. Human milk is also full of docosahexaenoic acid (DHA), an essential omega 3 fatty acid. DHA promotes brain and eye development. It also contains the carbohydrate, lactose. This promotes intestinal bacterial growth in the gut, which is important for digestion.

Breast milk is species specific. This is my favorite argument for nursing our babies. Each mammal mama produces milk that provides everything her babies need. For example, polar bear and whale milk is higher in fat because those animals need more fat to survive. Human milk is specifically designed for what the human baby needs. Formula made from cow's milk is not, however, it is perfect for baby cows.

Breastfed babies have less diarrhea. This is literally a life saver in developing countries where water sources and supplies are not clean and diarrhea is the leading cause of death in infants and small children.

Breastfed infants have fewer respiratory illnesses, allergies, asthma, diabetes, ear infections, Sudden Infant Death Syndrome (SIDS), Crohn's disease, and increased IQ and emotional security.

Suckling at the breast strengthens facial muscles and helps to align the baby's teeth better. This promotes better speech development and less need for orthodontics.

Breast milk contains endorphins, which are natural pain killers. This helps babies to cope with medical procedures, vaccines, bumps, and bruises.

Benefits to Mom

The process of developing breast milk and nursing benefits mothers physically and emotionally. The act of breastfeeding supports a mother's body as it shifts from pregnancy to the post-partum period. As a woman breastfeeds her baby, oxytocin is released, which causes the uterus to contract, bringing it back to its non-pregnant size sooner. This protects moms from postpartum hemorrhage and may result in less blood loss during the days after birth. Oxytocin also promotes relaxation, bonding with your baby, and reduces the risk of postpartum depression.

Producing breast milk burns calories, resulting in more weight loss. You can lose up to about 2 pounds a month just through nursing alone.

Breastfeeding also provides benefits that continue throughout a woman's lifetime, long after she weans her baby. A woman's iron levels can decrease during pregnancy, childbirth, and the postpartum period due to blood loss. The lack of periods caused by breastfeeding allows a woman's iron levels to recover, decreasing the chance of anemia. Breastfeeding decreases the risk of breast cancer occurring before menopause and adds protection from ovarian cancer. Giving your baby breast milk can decrease your risk of osteoporosis later in life. Even though calcium levels drop while nursing, your bone mineral content improves.

The emotional benefits are less tangible. There are no tests or labs to quantify how advantageous they are to mom. But it's the emotional benefits that can remind mom why humans are meant to breastfeed. One of my favorite perks of breastfeeding was the fact that I had to STOP to do it. It forced me to focus, relax, and connect with my babies when things were getting too rushed or chaotic (as will happen with a new baby!).

Breastfeeding is convenient. There are no bottles, or formula packs to lug around! "Have boobs, will travel!" As soon as your baby shows signs of hunger, you can nurse without having to prepare anything or make your baby wait. And, it is always fresh.

Breast milk is FREE!

Breastfeeding delays the return of your period after delivery. Therefore, breastfeeding can be used as birth control if you are exclusively breastfeeding your baby. Indeed, this was one of the best forms of birth control and child spacing back in the day. More information about breastfeeding and birth control can be found in Chapter 9.

There is a bonding that takes place while nursing your baby that can't be replicated by any other activity the two of your do. You are more aware of your baby's needs because you are holding your baby more and because your body is more connected to your baby. (Sometimes your body knows your baby needs to nurse before you have a chance to observe your baby's hunger cues: the heaviness of your breasts can be your first clue.) Your baby comes to rely on you for nourishment and comfort. Of course, dads can have a connection with their babies that is full of love and tenderness. But breastfeeding provides a bond between mom and baby that is just a little different and that much more special.

Benefits to Dad/Partner

Sure, Mom is the one who breastfeeds the baby, but dads and partners also benefit from the breastfeeding relationship. A breastfed baby is a healthier baby. This can greatly reduce stress for new parents, especially dads who feel pressure to be the "provider". Since breastfeeding also supports mom's health and well being, a partner can go to work knowing that the family is healthy and doing the best thing to help them stay that way.

Breast milk is FREE! (This is worth repeating.)

Dads can be available during the night for diaper changes, and to support Mom when she needs it.

Last, but maybe not least, breast milk poops are less stinky. This was my husband's favorite benefit!

Benefits to Society

Though the breastfeeding relationship lasts only a few months or years, the benefits last a lifetime for the mom, baby, family, and society. It has a ripple effect. A mom and her baby are healthier, thus her family stays well. Healthier babies become hearty adults. This results in fewer healthcare costs and more vigorous, happier people in our society.

Breastfeeding is also eco-friendly. Breastfeeding produces less consumer waste, which is better for the environment. Really, there is no waste with nursing. Only when mom is pumping is there the potential for waste. However, this is minimal compared to the waste when using formula.

Breastfeeding is good for business. There is less work absenteeism due to less illness. A more productive work force creates a better domestic economy. Now we just need to get the work place to better support moms who are pumping at work. This is slowly happening.

All of these benefits increase the longer a baby is breastfed!

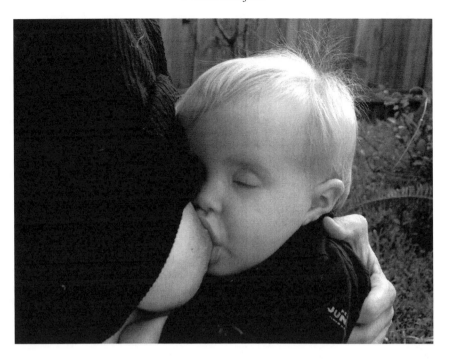

Chapter 2
Visualize It!
Benefits of Affirmations and Visualization

• • • • • • • • • • • •

My baby gains weight feeding only from my breasts.

MANY OF YOU MAY have heard of or even taken a hypnobirthing class during your pregnancy. I took one during my second pregnancy. In the class we learned coping techniques to handle the discomfort of labor, including visualizations. I was given a CD (really showing my age here) that had a visualization exercise on it, as well as many affirmations. I listened to this CD many nights before I went to bed and during my labor. This kept me grounded, kept my mind free of fear and focused on the wonderful, yet challenging thing I was doing. That experience inspired me to write a breastfeeding book incorporating visualization and affirmation. I feel that there is a need for this type of book because so many women are plagued with doubt and fear when it comes to nursing their baby. We have lost touch with our instinct to breastfeed because we are in our heads. Too much technology, a fast paced schedule, and no experience watching other women nurse have left us with an intellectual understanding of what breastfeeding is supposed to be, rather than an instinctual knowledge of what breastfeeding just is.

Visualization and affirmations will help you successfully breastfeed. Visualization is the act of seeing in your mind's eye the outcome you desire from any situation. Affirmations are positive statements you say to yourself that create a change in your attitude. I believe that visualization and affirmations are pivotal in creating success within us so that we create success in our world. This is true in all aspects of life, and can be used to create a successful breastfeeding experience for mom and baby.

When my mother introduced me to visualizing, I didn't welcome the idea with open arms. In fact, I really wanted nothing to do with it. I thought it was silly, far-fetched, and I was a little embarrassed for my mom. My mom made tapes of her own voice reciting visualization exercises and affirmations. She often listened to them as she was falling asleep at night. My brother and I would openly mock these. All of this was beyond me. Really, how could visualizing a ride along the colors of a rainbow make any difference in my life? I didn't get it, until I was a few years older.

I felt stressed about school and the constant fighting that went on between my brother and me. I developed migraines. As anyone who has experienced migraines knows, the pain is excruciating at times. Rather than ask my mom to chop my head off to ease the pain (which always seems like a good idea when I have a migraine), I asked her to give me one of her visualization tapes. For years she told me how the exercises could put a person into a deep state of relaxation, as if their body was floating away. I was feeling desperate, so I started to listen to my mom's visualization tapes as a way to relax and get over my headaches. The exercises weren't really focused on anything in particular; it was my mom's calm voice telling me to get more and more relaxed as I walked down the ocean shore. Her voice guided me along the shoreline and into a deeper state of calm.

So how does all this work? Have you ever wanted something so badly that you could see it actually becoming a reality? That's the power of visualization. Visualizing something isn't just about wanting it or wishing for it. It's about changing your thought pattern so that you BELIEVE your visualization as truth. You can't deny the truth, can you?

How do you go about changing your thought pattern? Seeing is believing. Whatever it is you are out to achieve, you have to see it as your reality. See it as happening, in the present, not in the future. For example, if you want a natural, unmedicated birth, visualize yourself actually laboring free of drugs, with your support people next to you. See and feel your strength. Watch yourself in your mind's eye achieving your goal as it is happening. Changing your thought pattern changes your attitude.

Don't visualize in terms of the future. In the above example, you wouldn't say to yourself, "I hope I can give birth without drugs" or "I'm going to try to give birth without drugs". This is nonproductive for two reasons:

1) Hoping something happens is putting the event in the future and allowing some uncertainty. We don't know what the future holds, which means that your event may or may not happen. There should be no question that it will happen, and no question of your success.

2) Proclaiming that you will try to do something allows room and gives permission for failure. Sure you can try, and you may succeed. Or you may not. See? You don't want to give failure or doubt a place in your visualizations, because visualizations are to bring you success.

I have experienced the power of visualization many times in my life. I will give you two examples. I studied the Russian language in college while the Iron Curtain was still in place. It wasn't a place I could go to for a vacation to practice my new language skills. So I signed up to go with a theater group (I was studying theater at the time). That didn't work out. I looked for a job there. That didn't work either. But I knew I was going to Russia somehow. I just KNEW. About 10 years and a career change to healthcare later, after the Soviet Union became Russia, I found an internship for aspiring midwives located in St. Petersburg. I wasn't looking for an internship and I certainly wasn't looking for a chance to go to Russia in that internet search, but it popped up just the same. I lived there for 3 months during the summer of 2000 and it was everything I wanted.

You may be saying to yourself, "Ha, it took her 10 years to get to Russia! That's too long to wait for a visualization to work." But during those 10 years, I still saw myself in Russia. I surrounded myself with Russian culture whenever I could. I made friends with native Russians and continued to practice the language. I saw myself in Russia all the time. The internship that took me there was so enriching that I believe it was the perfect way for me to go for what I wanted to do in my life. It wasn't just a vacation in Russia. It was a chance to actually live and work in Russia and experience everyday life. That trip combined two of my passions. If I had gone 10 years earlier, it wouldn't have been the right time for me to achieve my ultimate goals. Things really do happen when they are supposed to.

Another example is from my dating years. I went on many dates, most of them total bombs. I didn't feel a spark with the guy who was getting over a stomach bug, who instead of rescheduling our first date, came along and threw up in my car. I wasn't interested in the frat boy who got so drunk that I left him on the doorstep of his apartment- or what he thought was his apartment. And I didn't think I had a future with the lawyer who argued with *everything* I said. I went on so many blind dates that I actually ran out of friends to set me up. So, on the suggestion of a friend, (a fellow visualizer) I made a list of what I really wanted in a mate. It included some of the basic requirements: responsible with a good job, funny, good kisser. It also included some pretty specific things such as speaks another language, makes travel a top priority in life, and has a close relationship with his mother. I put the list away and never looked at it again. In fact, I forgot all about it, until I met Leon. After we dated for a couple of months, I remembered the list and looked it over. Leon had almost every trait on there, including the ones listed above. Of course, now he is my husband.

For most of my adult life, I have believed that "the subconscious is a yes machine". I first heard this idea in *Your Heart's Desire* by Sonia Choquette. The idea is that your subconscious backs up whatever you tell it, the ultimate supporter. Just make sure you are giving it something good to support. For instance, if you say to yourself, "I am wonderful," your subconscious says, "YES, I am!" But if you say, "I am a loser," your subconscious also says, "YES, I am!" in an equally enthusiastic voice. (I always imagine that my subconscious is very enthusiastic.) Creating positive visualizations about success happening in the present will be supported wholeheartedly by your subconscious.

Once you start making visualization a part of your daily routine, you will notice a change in your attitude. You feel more positive and more confident because you are in control of your life's path. Your visualizations create your reality. As your confidence grows and you see the results of your visualizations, you will know that anything is possible! What do you want for yourself? What do you want your experience to be? SEE IT. Visualize it.

AFFIRMATIONS

I love affirmations, but the love affair took a while to blossom. My mother also introduced me to affirmations. She had post-it notes of affirmations all over her bedroom and bathroom mirror. At the time, I was a cynical young tween and thought that my mother was a little kooky. "I am rich!" "I am healthy." "I deserve abundance." I rolled my eyes whenever I read them. I just didn't see how reading a sentence or two, no matter how positive or persuasive it may be, could change one's future. I thought my mom's belief in affirmations was out in la-la land.

In my mid-twenties, I got really into self-help books and rediscovered the idea of affirmations. Suddenly, it clicked. I realized that I was getting stuck in negative thinking. I wasn't a sour puss all of the time, but I was focusing on why I didn't have something, and believing that I would never get it. Instead, I needed to stop focusing on my lack of something, and start focusing on my abundance of it, even if I didn't have an abundance at the moment. Affirmations were constant positive messages of what could be coming my way. Who wouldn't benefit from that? So I hung affirmations all over my apartment, much like my mother did. Only, instead of post-it notes, I went all out and used colorful construction paper. My favorite was one I put on the back of my front door, so it was the last thing I saw on my way out to meet the world. "I deserve love."

Affirmations also helped me get through midwifery school, particularly on the really hard days when my self esteem was deflated. I had a deck of cards with affirmations written on them. I read one each morning after my shower and carried that message with me all day. Some days, I repeated the affirmation a hundred times!

Why is such a simple thing so powerful and effective? It's the idea of your subconscious being a "yes" machine. The affirmation gives you a positive message and your subconscious says "YES! That's true!" Your thoughts and attitude start to change, which change your actions. Now you are on your way to getting your way.

Some examples of affirmations for breastfeeding are:

I effortlessly latch my baby onto my breast.

I feel relaxed when my baby is nursing.

My milk is rich and abundant.

Nursing my baby is what my breasts are intended to do.

Can you see how saying these sentences over and over again could start to change your thinking? They may be even more powerful if you write your own.

PRACTICE MAKES A PERFECT LIFE

Pregnancy, labor, birth, and breastfeeding are such wonderful stages in a woman's life to practice visualization and affirmation. We all have strong ideas of how we want these events to play out. Unfortunately, in our modern life of fast-paced technology, over-scheduling and lack of community, it's too easy to deny our inner voice, the one that knows our body is strong enough and made for these stages. Fear can creep in and create negativity. This is not what you need when you are birthing or nursing your baby.

In the childbirth class I teach, I explain how visualization and affirmation can foster a satisfying birth experience and breastfeeding success. I have the students sit comfortably in a chair or lie down on the floor; I dim the lights. After they have relaxed and focused on their breathing, I guide them through a visualization of their birth or breastfeeding experience. Here is what some of the moms I worked with have to say about it:

> "I found the visualization tools to be incredibly helpful. When breastfeeding was painful in the beginning, and when I was feeding my daughter through a bout of mastitis, I would often use visualization to redirect my energies and relax."

> "While in labor I used visualization to stay calm. I visualized the baby coming down. I also visualized my favorite place, which is my grandma's house. Seeing myself play in the sand at her house helped to stay positive and relaxed. It also kept my mind off of the contractions. During labor I repeated 'relax' and 'I can do this'. It was very rhythmic and helped to keep me calm and focused."

> "While I was still pregnant, I would often visualize breastfeeding going well. I believe in the mind/body connection and I do think that everything in my birth went according to my "plan" and, therefore, my visualization."

One doula who also attended my class now uses visualization and affirmations with her clients.

> "The visualization exercises from your class are wonderful because they are guided. So often, visualization can be quite random. I have used them for several of my clients and they love it. It really prepares the mind."

Visualizing success can bring success into all aspects of your life. It can improve your love life, your financial situation, your job success, and your mental and physical health. Trusting your body is the first step to breastfeeding success. Don't say to yourself, "I am going to try to nurse my baby and see how it goes." If you want to nurse your baby, then believe that you can do it. Period. "I am nursing my baby and it is effortless." Visualize yourself already nursing your baby and make it a reality. Affirmations are an effective way to create confidence in our ability to give our babies what they need. Find a way to carve time out of your day to make visualizing and affirming your beliefs a daily practice. It will make all the difference.

Visualize It!

Visualization exercises can be found at the end of each chapter. Affirmations are included throughout the book and a complete list of them can be found in Appendix 1. These will help you picture yourself as a breastfeeding mother before you actually do it. What you visualize now becomes your reality later. Often, when I ask my prenatal clients if they plan to breastfeed, they answer, "I hope to" or "If I can, yes." Well, why wouldn't she be able to breastfeed her baby? This woman already doubts the whole process before she even starts. That isn't the foundation for successful breastfeeding; it allows failure to be an option. Visualization is more than imagining a situation. It is playing out the scenario in your mind, seeing the success of your actions. This success becomes implanted in your subconscious. Visualizing successful breastfeeding creates a positive image of you nursing your baby in your subconscious. Whatever your subconscious believes to be true becomes the truth for you. Visualization is a powerful tool for creating success in any aspect of your life including preparation for the birth of your baby.

When you do a visualization exercise, it helps to be in a relaxed state of mind. Sit comfortably or lie down in a quiet, dark room. Some people prefer to listen to soft music. You might have someone read the exercise aloud to you while you relax with your eyes closed. Allow yourself this time with no distractions from the outside world. Let the others in your home know that you are not to be disturbed for the next 15 minutes (or however long you decide to do this.) Turn off the ringer to your phone.

The exercises are meant to offer suggestions of images to conjure in your mind. Read through the visualization first to get an idea of the theme you want to focus on. Then close your eyes and envision what the scenario looks like with you as the main character. For example, if the exercise is about latching the baby onto your breast, imagine yourself actually latching your baby onto your breast. That's it. There are no rules about this: only that you picture whatever you are doing in a positive way. Your body is producing milk, and your baby is nursing beautifully. If you start to feel fear or doubt, stop and open your eyes, so the movie in your mind "stops" and you can edit as needed. Then close your eyes again. Try to refocus on the positive image and begin again. If doubt continues, try to continue the scenario while you work through the obstacle you are experiencing. Use the visualization to "see" yourself finding a solution to the problem and move on from there. This can be helpful to turn your negative feelings such as doubt and fear into positive ones. Let your imagination run wild and "see" you and your baby successfully breastfeeding!

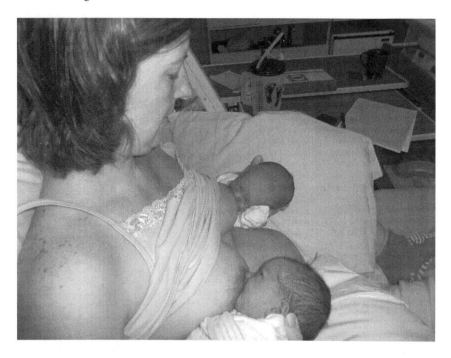

Chapter 3
Successful Breastfeeding Before The Birth

• • • • • • • • • • •

I love to nurse my baby!

WHERE YOU GIVE BIRTH has an impact on your breastfeeding success. Are you giving birth to your baby in a hospital, a birth center, or at home? How did you come to that decision? Many couples make this decision based on how they feel about natural birth, pain medication, and the potential unknowns of birthing. Your birthing place and providers influence your labor and birth experience. For example, does your provider stay with you when you are in labor, or does she come at the end when the baby is crowning? Are pain medications an option in your place of birth or will you rely on other comfort measures to handle labor discomfort?

Your choice of birth place also affects your early breastfeeding experience. Does your place of birth keep moms and babies together unless it's medically necessary to separate them? Are babies taken to the nursery at night? Are pacifiers and bottles of formula given to babies without parents' permission? Is your provider available to help you nurse right after birth? Are there lactation consultants on staff? Do your providers and their assistants feel as strongly about breastfeeding as you do?

While you and your baby are figuring this whole nursing thing out, you don't want anyone to give your baby a pacifier or bottle. This can affect how your baby latches to your breast, and will affect your milk supply. Nobody should be offering anything to your baby without your consent.

If you will be giving birth in a hospital, it's a good idea to ask your provider ahead of time how she feels about breastfeeding, how the nurses on staff feel about breastfeeding (they will be with you much more than your provider), and what kind of breastfeeding support you will have while in the hospital and after you go home. Some hospitals are Baby Friendly. If you are delivering in a Baby Friendly hospital, you can rest assured that the staff will be knowledgeable and supportive of breastfeeding, but still let them know what your desires are.

For a hospital to be Baby Friendly, it must adhere to a specific set of standards, as outlined by UNICEF/WHO (World Health Organization). (5) For the United States, these are:

- Maintain a written breastfeeding policy that is routinely communicated to all health care staff.

- Train all health care staff in skills necessary to implement this policy.

- Inform all pregnant women about the benefits and management of breastfeeding.

- Help mothers initiate breastfeeding within one hour of birth.

- Show mothers how to breastfeed and how to maintain lactation, even if they are separated from their infants.

- Give infants no food or drink other than breast milk, unless medically indicated.

- Practice "rooming in", allow mothers and infants to remain together 24 hours a day.

- Encourage unrestricted breastfeeding.

- Give no pacifiers or artificial nipples to breastfeeding infants.

- Foster the establishment of breastfeeding support groups and refer mothers to them upon discharge from the hospital.

You can search for a Baby Friendly hospital online.

If you are having an out of hospital birth in a free standing birth center or in your home, you are most likely working with a midwife or doctor who is supportive of natural, unmedicated birth, as well as breastfeeding. It may seem obvious that your provider will offer help when needed, but it's still a good idea to talk to her about her feelings towards nursing and what kind of support she offers after the baby is born.

If you are reading this book and have already delivered your baby, think about the support you received and what kind of help was available. This may make a difference in where you birth in the future, should you have another baby.

Get Your Team Together

Think about how you feel about breastfeeding your baby. What does that mean to you? Is it simply feeding your baby or does it have a deeper meaning to you? (There are no right answers to these questions.) Once you have assessed your feelings, it's time to get your team together. Who will be your support around breastfeeding? What are your partner's feelings about breastfeeding? Do you have relatives or friends who have breastfed in the past? Will they provide you with support and encouragement? Is your midwife or doctor pro-breastfeeding? Is the place where you birth supportive of your success? These people will be the ones to encourage, support, help and listen when things are tough in the beginning. Knowing who you can count on before you need help can save you time and energy.

Visualization & Affirmation

Start to visualize and affirm your breastfeeding success while you are still pregnant. I recommend doing the visualization exercises daily, either before bed, or when you have some quiet time alone during the day. Repeat the affirmations to yourself throughout your day. Maybe even write them down and hang them on the wall, your bathroom mirror, or in the car. Put them some where you will see them easily and often. These will be a constant reminder that your body knows how to produce milk and nourish your baby.

Writing Your Birth Plan

A birth plan puts your desires in writing. It puts everyone involved in your birth on the same page. Some of the things you might include in your birth plan seem obvious, like "I don't want a C-section". I think most of us would agree that we don't want that! But rather than just stating the obvious, think about what you really want, what you really don't, and what you will accept if offered for medical reasons. Include your desires regarding the birth, baby care, and breastfeeding. Though you have written down what you want, nothing is written in stone. Don't get so caught up in the "perfect" plan, in case things need to change while in labor. Your desires may change during the process or a medical reason may necessitate deviating from the original plan.

Try to keep your birth plan as simple and as short as possible while making all of your wishes known. One to two pages is a good length; you aren't writing a book. Appendix 2 has a list of questions for you and your partner to discuss when writing your birth plan.

Hiring a Doula

A doula is a trained and experienced professional who provides physical and emotional support to a pregnant woman and her partner during the prenatal, labor and birth, and postpartum period. She is not medical staff, and she does not replace your provider. She does not make medical decisions for you. Rather, she helps you make your decisions by providing information, education, and support. She acts as an advocate for her client, ensuring that her client is having the birth experience she desires while still maintaining a safe environment for her and the baby. Her services can be invaluable to a family. She provides support during the birth process by providing comfort measures to the laboring woman, making sure she eats and drinks, and gives her constant encouragement. She often helps with breastfeeding at postpartum visits, or can watch the baby while mom gets some rest. She can even do a load of laundry and cook dinner!

Doulas also do not take the place of any family or friends you want at your birth. Of course, nothing can replace your loved ones. Sometimes they are the ones who make you feel the safest in any situation. They are very invested in you, your baby, and your experience. Your doula is also invested in this without the same emotional attachment. Sometimes, having that emotional distance can allow the doula to see things differently and assist you in making better decisions for yourself. I have met many doulas in my career, and each one has a special passion about supporting a woman during labor and birth and through her transition to motherhood.

Studies have shown that doulas can positively affect the birth outcome. Labors attended by a doula tend to be shorter in duration, result in fewer interventions such as forceps, vacuum extraction, and cesarean section, and require less pain medication. (6) Doulas can be even more beneficial if you are having a hospital birth. While in the hospital, your birth experience is affected by hospital protocols and rules. A doula experienced in hospital births can help you navigate these rules so that you can still have the birth experience you desire.

Decide what you want your experience to be and then interview several doulas to see who is a good match for you and your partner. A doula should be experienced and confident in the birth and breastfeeding process, but not so overpowering that she makes your experience her experience. I had 3 doulas at my first daughter's birth, two were midwife friends and the third was a doula we hired. We always joke that my husband had 2 doulas and I had one. It felt like a big party. You could feel everyone's excitement in the air for the birth of our baby. Each doula had strengths that came into play when I needed them most. I could not imagine that birth without each person there.

For my second daughter's birth, I hired the same doula as before (she has become a friend). The other two friends had moved to different states, but I also felt that I wanted a quieter experience for this birth and less of a party atmosphere. My doula, my husband, and my midwife provided all the support I needed. It was a wonderful experience. Though they were very different, I felt very supported both times. My husband was thrilled that I wanted to have doulas at both births. He felt relieved that he wasn't my only support person, since he had never been to a birth before. It has always seemed odd to me that we expect the husbands and partners to be the major support person at a birth. Most of the time, men have no experience to prepare them for the life altering experience of birth. I think it is wonderful that men are in the birthing rooms, rather than the waiting rooms, but it's a lot of pressure for us to expect him to put aside his emotions and be the sole support person for a laboring mom. A doula can take that pressure off of him and offer him emotional support too. A doula can also make sure he doesn't forget to rest, eat and drink during the whole experience.

Once home, the doula watched the baby while I slept and she made us dinner a few nights. And yes, despite my training and experience, I needed some help with baby care. The doulas I used were also moms and I loved getting their tried and true advice. The doula you use for birth will come to your house once or twice after the baby is born to help with baby care, breastfeeding and to discuss your birth experience. Not every labor doula does postpartum visits. There are some doulas that only do postpartum work and do not attend births. If consistency is important to you, find a doula that does both and book her!

When interviewing a doula, you want to know that she has a similar philosophy about childbirth and baby care. Some questions to ask are:

- What is your birth philosophy? How will you support us if our decisions are not the same as yours?
- What is your training? Are you certified?
- What is your experience?
- How often do you meet with us before/after the birth?
- When would you join me in labor?
- Do you work with backup doulas? Can we meet them?
- Do you meet with us to review a birth plan before the birth? Do you meet with us after the birth to review and answer any questions we have about the experience?
- Do you do regular post partum visits?
- What is your fee?

Resources to help you find a doula are listed in the back of the book.

Got Supplies?

Before your baby arrives, take the time to think about what supplies you may need for breastfeeding. Will you need a pump? What kind of pump? Do your research ahead of time to find the one that will best match your needs. Be sure to also purchase bottles for storing your expressed breast milk. Other items you may want to have on hand before the baby is born are nursing bras, nursing pads, lanolin, slings, and nursing shirts (these have slits in them to make your breast more easily accessible.)

Talk to a Lactation Consultant

Many women will not need a lactation consultant because they will have no issues with breastfeeding, but it's a good idea to know how to contact one if the need arises. The last thing you want is to be tired and frustrated and worried about your baby's feeding or your milk supply and feel like you don't know where to turn for help. You may want to consider talking to a lactation consultant while you are still pregnant if you know there is an issue, such as inverted nipples or previous breast surgery. A lactation consultant can educate you on what to expect when your baby is born, how to manage some common obstacles, and how to get your baby on your breast.

To find a lactation consultant in your area, search the database of the International Lactation Consultant Association, which can be found online.

Visualize It!

You have just given birth and put your baby to your breast for the first time. See your support people and loved ones around you. Notice the light in the room. Hear the music if you have any playing. Feel the gentle tug of your baby's suckle. It's strong, but comfortable! Notice how perfectly your bodies fit together, regardless of the position you are nursing in. Your partner or support person climbs into the bed with you (or pulls a chair next to your bed) so he or she can witness what is happening. You both marvel at how quickly your baby has figured out what to do! Your baby has nursed for a while and seems very satisfied. When she pulls herself off the breast, you notice some colostrum left on her lips and your nipple. You give your breast tissue a gentle squeeze and see more colostrum expressed. Your body is producing exactly what it should: the perfect amounts for your newborn.

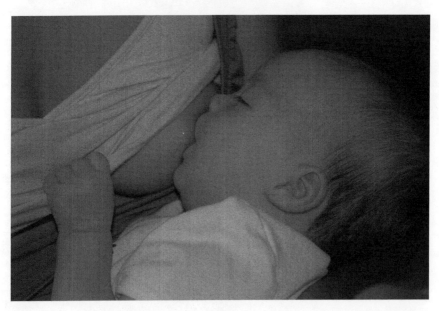

Amy's Thoughts

I wanted to breastfeed because it seemed to fulfill this romantic part of motherhood. I never considered not nursing. It seemed so tender, something to do with your child. It seemed so special to me. As the due date got closer, I got more excited and looked forward to breastfeeding. It was another rite of passage that women get to do.

I was nervous to breastfeed, nervous and excited, because I had friends who had problems with it. Now that I've done it, I'm very happy and feel fortunate that it was easy for me. I almost felt aroused and would tingle with happiness when I breastfed. I felt so close to Evie and was really proud of myself for doing it.

I suspect Evie saw me as her main provider for a long time and preferred me to her dad. I don't know if that would have been the same if I hadn't breastfed. I think she has instinctive knowledge that I fed her for a long time.

I just loved the closeness we had when I nursed. My baby had this face when she was done breastfeeding, and no one saw that face but me.

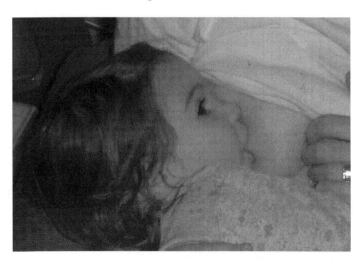

Chapter 4
What Are My Breasts Doing?

∙ ∙ ∙ ∙ ∙ ∙ ∙ ∙ ∙ ∙ ∙ ∙

My milk is laying down the foundation
for optimal health of my baby.

You have probably noticed quite a few changes to your breasts recently. The function of your breasts is to produce milk for your baby. They were *literally* made to breastfeed. They start to prepare for this big job the minute you become pregnant. Many people believe that breastfeeding is responsible for the way your breasts look after you have babies (a little lower to the ground and a little softer than before). In reality, the changes that will affect the look of your breasts happen during your pregnancy, whether you breastfeed or not.

What exactly are these changes? Well, for one, they are bigger! This is how you know your body is getting pumped for producing milk (get the pun?!?). In fact, if you haven't noticed a change in your breasts, discuss this with your midwife or doctor. In rare cases, it can mean a problem that will prevent a woman from producing milk.

Some changes can be seen, some can be felt. You may not notice all of them, but all are important. The areola, or dark area around your nipple, has gotten even darker, due to the increase in estrogen. Babies have very poor vision at birth (smell is their strongest sense). This contrast in color helps the baby to see your nipple better. The Montgomery tubercles, the glands around your nipple, become more prominent. As mentioned before, these lubricate your nipples to protect the skin from dryness while nursing. Your nipples are more sensitive due to the increase in estrogen. An increase in blood flow to your breasts may produce visible veins. These will go away after you deliver.

What changes have you noticed in your breasts since you became pregnant?

Basic Anatomy & Physiology

Breasts are made mostly of fat and connective tissue, rather than glandular tissue (which is responsible for milk production). Therefore, size doesn't matter. A small breast has the potential to have the same amount of glandular tissue as a large breast. The storage space for milk inside the breast is not related to breast size. The outside of your breast is made up of the nipple, areola (the area of darker skin) and Montgomery tubercles (the bumpy part of the areola).

Inside your breasts is a ductile system, busy at work producing and delivering milk for your baby. The ducts run from the end of your nipple inward, leading to the alveoli. Alveoli are milk producing cells that release milk into the ducts surrounding the nipple. The alveoli form clusters like bunches of grapes and are made of different types of cells, which synthesize fat and protein into milk and contract to eject the milk into the ductile system. The milk follows a path until it finds its way through the pores of the nipple. During suckling, milk is ejected into the lactiferous ducts (milk ducts) which are connected to the nipple. This is how milk gets from the inside of your breast to the outside. Milk is stored in these ducts inbetween and during the breastfeeding session.

When the baby suckles, he is compressing the lactiferous ducts by drawing the nipple and areola into his mouth. This causes the nipple to elongate up to twice its normal length. The act of suckling expresses the milk from your nipple to his mouth. By the way, you have many openings in your nipple, not just one like a rubber nipple. I have worked with many moms and dads who were shocked to see their milk spray all over the place! My husband was so impressed by the power of my "spray" that he would often request a demo after my daughter nursed.

The Key Players: Prolactin & Oxytocin

There are many hormones involved in the symphony of producing milk for your baby, but the stars of the show are prolactin and oxytocin.

Milk production starts once the placenta is delivered (though colostrum, the first milk your body produces for your baby, is produced during pregnancy).

This is when the estrogen and progesterone levels decrease and the prolactin levels increase. However, prolactin levels gradually decrease over time during the lactation process.

Prolactin is produced by the anterior pituitary gland and is responsible for the production of milk. It is released once the baby has begun suckling from his mother's breast. Suckling also increases the levels of prolactin, which positively affects milk production. Increased amounts of prolactin also prevent ovulation, which is why most breastfeeding moms experience a delay in their periods after they deliver.

Oxytocin is produced by the posterior pituitary gland and is responsible for the release of milk. It causes the ductile system in the breast to contract. This is known as the milk ejection reflex, or "letdown". Oxytocin levels can rise without a baby suckling the breast. This is why a woman can have a letdown when she isn't with her baby, but has heard another baby crying. Or she can have a letdown by just thinking of her baby. Relaxation aids the letdown, while stress and tension inhibit it. It's important to find a relaxing time and place to nurse or pump, so that you can offer the most milk possible to your baby.

While nursing, your baby will compress the areola with her gums, releasing oxytocin and causing a letdown. Without letdown, milk will not be delivered from the aveoli to the milk ducts. The sensation of letdown has been described as tingling, pressure, or discomfort. To me, letdown felt like a sudden flood of milk running through the inside of my breasts. I would imagine a rapid flash flood like a river running through a canyon or a large waterfall inside my breasts. You will find your own analogy to describe what you are feeling. Some women don't ever feel a letdown sensation, but it is still happening.

Oxytocin also causes the uterus to contract (you experienced this during labor) so you will feel contractions while nursing the first few days after delivery. Don't worry, they are nothing compared to your labor contractions. Oxytocin is also released during orgasm, which is why it has been called the pleasure hormone. If oxytocin is released during orgasm, and milk is released by oxytocin... You guessed it: you might have a spray of milk during your orgasm! While some people might find this amusing, I know others will find it embarrassing. We will talk more about sexuality in Chapter 9.

Visualize It!

Imagine your hormones talking to each other, each giving the signal to produce milk for your baby. Picture this any way that works for you. Are your hormones actually speaking to each other? Are they sending musical notes to each other to get the message across? Maybe your hormones sing together in perfect harmony like a choir. Or is it a silent communication? Maybe your hormones rise together like a tide in the moonlight. As they do your breasts expand and fill with milk. Maybe they illuminate together like brilliant stars. See how this message affects your breast tissue, making it expand and fill with more milk. Imagine the milk ducts in your breasts filling with milk. You may feel a tingling sensation when you do this exercise illustrating the strong connection between our minds and our bodies.

Betsy's Thoughts

I wanted to breastfeed because I kept hearing how it was the best food for my baby. As a biology teacher, it made sense to me. I'm a mammal and that's what we do: nurse our babies. Breastfeeding is the root of being a mammal. I didn't like the idea of giving my baby formula, something that was made from cow's milk, not human milk.

Before I had my baby, I heard that breastfeeding was not the easiest thing. But I didn't know it could be as agonizing as it was. Early on it was hard and painful and I think I wanted to quit. But I had lots of encouragement from my partner. I never had to ask for anything; she just knew when to help me out. She would bring me pillows before I needed them, and get me outside support from friends and lactation consultants. Breastfeeding created a really, really strong bond with my baby, stronger than the bond with her other mom, even though she was her mom too.

Why did I keep going? My partner encouraged me as much as she could. I felt that I really wanted to do this for my baby. I also knew at some point it would kick in and wouldn't hurt anymore. I knew this from stories other moms told, and also because every once in a while, Georgia would latch on and it wouldn't hurt. So I thought we just had to figure out how to get that good latch again.

I would say to women who are having trouble at first to stick with it. For most people, it eventually works out. Georgia is 4 now and still nursing for comfort. I couldn't get started and now I can't stop! It took 14 weeks for me to get it right, but I'm really glad I did.

Chapter 5
Birth to Two Weeks

• • • • • • • • • • •

I am committed to giving my
baby milk from my breasts.

Now that your baby is born and in your arms, the real fun begins! The
first two weeks of your baby's life are spent with the family getting to know
this new person and vice versa. You have begun your "babymoon". It's a good
time to settle in at home without too many visitors or interruptions, so you
have the time and space to figure out how to be this "new" family. The first
two weeks are also the time when you are establishing your milk supply, so it
is extra important to focus on nursing, and learning your baby's cues.

First Feeding

The most important feeding in terms of establishing your milk supply
is the first feeding. This should happen within an hour of the birth of your
baby. Nursing within an hour of birth brings prolactin (the hormone that
produces milk) to its highest potential levels, higher than at any other time
during your breastfeeding relationship. This spike lays the foundation for your
future milk supply and breastfeeding success. If nursing is delayed past that
first hour, prolactin levels might not reach quite as high, which can prevent
future milk supply from being quite as abundant. Babies are also the most
alert and awake right after birth, so you want to seize this opportunity. After
that, they usually go into a sleepy state for the first twenty-four hours that can
make nursing more of a challenge.

Place your baby skin-to-skin (both of you topless) on your chest after the
birth. This will keep your baby warmer than any blanket or hospital warmer.

It will also allow her to smell your smell and hear your heart beat, which has comforted her for the last nine months. For that reason, it's best to nurse before the baby gets her first bath; a bath with soap might interfere with the baby's scent recognition of mom.

Make sure your support people, health care provider, and nurses know how important it is for your baby to nurse within an hour of her birth. Include it in your birth plan. If for some reason, you can't latch your baby on then, someone else can do it for you. After my first daughter was born, my placenta was taking a very long time to deliver. There was a lot going on "down there" to get my placenta out and much of it was painful for me, so I wasn't really in a place to help my daughter latch onto my breast. But I had a wonderful doula and she knew how important it was to me for my daughter to nurse within an hour of her birth. My doula latched her on and held her at my breast for her first feeding. I will always be grateful for that!

If for some reason you are not able to latch your baby on in the first hour, either because you had a cesarean section, or your baby was taken to the neonatal intensive care unit, or your baby just wouldn't latch on the first try, don't lose hope. If you are still with your baby, hold him on your chest skin-to-skin. This alone will positively affect your prolactin levels. Let your baby's hands touch or hold you breast. Try again when you and your baby are ready. If you are separated from your baby, start to pump with an electric double pump as soon as you can. Continue to pump at least every 3 hours until you and your baby are reunited.

Colostrum

Colostrum is liquid gold! It is the substance your body produces to feed your baby during the first 3-6 days after birth and before your milk comes in. It has a yellowish color from high levels of beta carotene, and is thinner than mature milk. (Mature milk is the milk your body produces after colostrum for the entire time you nurse.) Its production starts during the latter part of pregnancy. If you can express milk at the end of your pregnancy, it's colostrum. But don't worry. Even if your nipples are as dry as a desert in pregnancy, your body will know what to do after birth. The body starts to produce milk once the placenta is delivered, after estrogen levels decrease and prolactin levels increase. (This is why even mothers who deliver their babies very early still produce milk for them.)

Colostrum is very dense in calories, glucose, and nutrients. It is high in carbohydrates, protein, and antibodies, and low in fat. It contains antibodies and white blood cells, which come from you and fight off infection. Together these protect your baby from viruses and bacteria. Ingesting colostrum will establish the flora (good bacteria) of your baby's digestive tract, preventing the absorption of harmful substances and creating a healthier and more efficient digestive tract. This is one reason why breastfed babies have less gas and diarrhea.

Colostrum is also very low in volume. This low volume gets a lot of parents anxious that their baby is not getting enough to eat. Parents are worried that their baby is starving. NOT TRUE! Your baby has some fat stores left over from when she was inside of you, so she will not starve. The reason for colostrum's low volume is the baby's immature digestive system. Delivering the nutrients your baby needs in a low volume substance will create fewer digestive problems. Remember, your baby's stomach is very small. By day 1, your baby's stomach can hold about 5-7ml, which is about the size of a marble. By day 3, the capacity of your baby's stomach is an ounce, or the size of a shooter marble and by day 7, the stomach can hold about 1.5-2 oz, which is the size of a ping pong ball. If you give your baby more than her stomach can hold, she will spit up the excess. (7)

Colostrum also has a mild laxative effect which aids in the passing of your baby's first stool, known as meconium. Meconium contains high amounts of bilirubin, a waste product of broken down red blood cells. The passing of meconium will help to prevent jaundice, a symptom of increased amounts of bilirubin. One drop of colostrum is more concentrated with the good stuff than one drop of mature milk. Your baby gets more bang for her buck when she gets colostrum. I have seen many parents give their babies formula while still in the hospital because they were convinced that the baby was starving on colostrum only. No amount of educating could convince them otherwise. Of course, each parent has to do what they feel is best for their baby. However, giving your baby formula in this situation isn't necessarily the best idea. Formula may fill your baby's tummy, but you won't be filling it with optimal nutrition. And if your baby's tummy is too full of formula, she won't want to nurse as often. This will adversely affect your milk supply. Your body will think it doesn't need to make so much milk for a baby who doesn't nurse as often.

Premature babies benefit from colostrum even more. Special components of colostrum called growth modulators help the premature baby adjust to oral feedings. These babies will greatly benefit from the immune boosting property of colostrum. Premature babies also benefit greatly from skin-to-skin contact with their mothers while nursing. In fact, all babies benefit from this, but studies have been done specifically on premature babies, showing how skin-to-skin contact can reduce the length of the neonatal hospital stay and promote breastfeeding. (8) (9)

Sometimes a mom can't put her baby to her breast right away, but is still determined to give her baby only breast milk, including colostrum. To do this, she uses a pump. But the colostrum comes out in such small amounts, there isn't any in the bottle or bag she is using to collect her milk. What's a mom to do in this case? Ask your nurse, midwife, or doctor for some needleless syringes. Draw up the colostrum as it comes from your nipple and give it to your baby through the syringe. You can give your baby even a few drops this way, every bit is a huge benefit to her health.

It may take a few hours for the colostrum to come in after you deliver. This is normal. It's like ordering a pizza for delivery. The baby suckles at first, putting in the order. The body gets the message that it needs to start sending milk. The milk is delivered. Just like the pizza is delivered 45 minutes after you make the call.

After colostrum, what we think of as "breast milk" (also known as mature milk) comes in. Your milk will come in three-six days after birth. The more you nurse, the faster your milk will come in because you are sending a stronger message to your body that you've got a baby and she needs food!!! Often, this can cause a feeling of engorgement which usually lasts about forty-eight hours. This type of engorgement is usually caused by the inflammation of the breast tissue as it undergoes normal changes while your milk comes in. Heat packs on your breasts before you nurse and cold compresses on your breasts after you nurse can help with the discomfort. Really, this is just the time it takes your body to figure out what's going on and how to adjust for this new volume of milk.

Establishing Your Milk Supply

Sometimes, when breastfeeding moms think they don't have enough milk to feed their baby, they decide to supplement with formula. However, it is very rare for a mother to have insufficient milk if she breastfeeds exclusively, and on demand, from birth. Insufficient milk is usually caused by a medical condition. What is very common is for the mother's milk supply to decrease if she does not keep up the supply with the demand. This can be a big obstacle when mothers decide to go back to work or school if they don't keep up their pumping schedule.

Breastfeeding is all about *supply and demand*. Your baby provides the demand; your body produces the supply. *This is the key to maintaining your milk supply.*

How do you keep up with the demand? It is important to stimulate your breasts at least eight times in a twenty-four hour period, sending the message that milk needs to be produced. This translates to nursing or pumping about every three hours. Otherwise, your body thinks that you don't need to produce as much milk and your milk supply decreases. If you decide to give your baby a bottle, then you need to pump during that usual feeding time. Otherwise, your supply will go down. If you are at work or school for the day, you need to pump about every three hours to maintain your supply. You want your body to keep up with the same demand as if you were home with your baby.

So, should your baby be on a three hour feeding "schedule?" NO! It is more accurate to think of nursing at least eight times in a twenty-four hour period. That way if your baby gives you the gift of a four or five hour stretch of sleep at night, you may need to nurse more often during the day to get in eight feedings. These daytime feedings would be spaced together closer than every three hours.

If you give your baby anything other than the breast without pumping, your body will think it doesn't have to work as hard and *your milk supply will decrease*. I may sound like a broken record right now, but, in my experience, this is the most common reason moms have quit nursing. They think their supply has diminished so much that they can't feed their baby what he needs. I hear, "I have no milk" over and over again. Most likely the mom has milk (again, it's rare for a mother to have *no* milk). She probably has enough of a supply for the demand her body is aware of. It's just not the amount her baby would be demanding if he was at the breast more (or the mom was pumping more). If she nursed or pumped more often, she would see her supply increase.

It is possible for a mother to increase her supply after it has decreased by nursing or pumping more often. Spending a day snuggling with your baby skin-to-skin and offering the breast often can make a huge difference. However, you need to be committed. You may also need to nurse/pump more often than every three hours or take galactogogues. Galactogogues are foods, herbs, or drugs that aid in increasing your milk supply. A list of them can be found at the end of this book in Appendix 3.

Waking Your Baby

In the beginning, newborns don't have the same hunger stimuli that adults do. Sometimes we need to tell them it's time to eat. Even if a newborn is sleeping, you should wake him up to feed if it's been longer than three hours. Once your baby has returned to his birth weight and is growing well, you can just let your sleeping baby sleep.

It can be tricky to wake a newborn. They can sleep through anything except when you really need them to! Thankfully, there are some very effective ways of arousing them. First, take off all of his blankets so he isn't quite so snuggly and comfortable. Change your baby's diaper. It probably needs to be changed and this is hard to sleep through! If your baby is still sleepy, hold your baby in your arms in front of you with one hand under his head and the other supporting his body. (His body will be perpendicular to yours.) Swing him side to side and watch his eyes open. He may give you a little scowl for waking him! If he is at the breast and falling asleep, raise his outside arm over his head. Both of these actions stimulate the part of brain which arouses us. Don't continue to rock him as rocking puts babies to sleep.

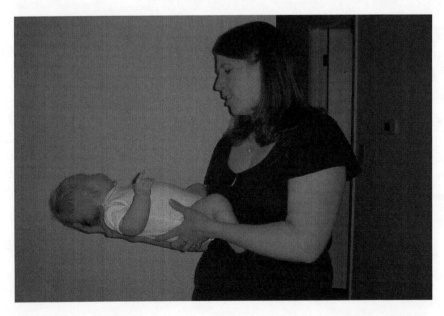

If all else fails, take a cold, wet washcloth and rub his face and tummy with it. Yikes! That will wake him up and make him MAD! He'll probably also be ready to nurse.

If your baby is falling asleep at the breast, it may be that he isn't getting much milk. Try compressing your breast tissue behind the areola in a "pumping" rhythm. This will express milk into your baby's mouth, keeping him interested. It's hard to sleep with your mouth full of milk.

Hunger Cues

How do you know your baby is hungry and ready to nurse? She will give you a few clues before she starts to cry over it, such as smacking her lips, sucking on her hands, and rooting. Rooting is the baby's instinct to move her head in the direction of the nipple, looking for it. This is most evident when her cheek is stroked. Of course, babies cry when they are hungry too. However, crying is your baby's last effort to get your attention, which usually means we missed the other cues. So we'd better get that baby fed!

Many moms are "wearing" their babies these days in the United States. This has been done for years in other countries, but is just starting to become more popular here. Wearing your baby in a wrap or a sling keeps him close so you can read his hunger cues earlier. This allows you to tend to his needs sooner, which often results in less crying. Babies who are worn also have less gas, and sleep more than babies who are left alone in a crib, swing, or bouncy chair. You can nurse while your baby is in the wrap or sling. This just takes some practice, but can make things much more convenient and discreet when out in public.

How do you know that your baby is full and not just "playing with your nipple"? Most babies will simply take themselves off of the breast when they are done. Your baby also won't root anymore. She will have a relaxed posture, her arms will be relaxed, her eyes may be closed. Most likely, she will fall asleep after nursing. Don't just let your baby "play with your nipple" as this will cause irritation and soreness. If your baby really needs to suckle for comfort, give her your clean finger to suck on for a while.

It Is Not Possible to Spoil Your Baby!

Your baby has spent the last nine months in contact with your body: a tight, dark, warm space. This new world she lives in is big, bright, and cold. Of course, she wants to snuggle with you to know that she is safe and taken care of! She needs to trust that you will provide whatever she needs and right now she needs as much love and affection as you can give.

During the newborn stage, a baby's needs are simply basic human needs: food, shelter (this includes the protective shelter of your arms), and warmth. You can't spoil someone by giving them basic human needs. If your baby wants to nurse more frequently than the average baby, it is important to acknowledge and grant these desires. It won't spoil your baby. It will build trust. When her needs are met, she will learn that she can trust you, which has long lasting positive effects on your relationship with her.

You might have someone in your life telling you that you are creating bad habits by holding your baby so much. I often hear this in reference to co-sleeping. Sleeping with your newborn won't last forever. I promise your kid will not want to sleep with you when she is in college! I encourage you to kiss, hug, and hold your baby as much as possible. Don't let anyone tell you to stop. They don't stay babies forever, and before you know it your daughter will be more interested in talking on the phone to her friends than talking to you, and your son will be too cool to kiss his mom.

When Do I Breastfeed?

When should you offer your breast to your baby? Whenever she asks. Nurse at least eight times in a twenty-four hour period to maintain your supply and keep your baby satisfied. However, each baby is different and you will soon learn what your baby's feeding patterns are. Some babies want to feed more often than three hours. This could be because your breasts have a smaller storage capacity and your baby gets smaller amounts of milk more often. A woman's storage capacity is not necessarily related to her breast size. I am overflowing with breast tissue, yet, my daughter needed to nurse every two hours. This could be because I stored less milk for each feeding so she had to nurse more often. Or it could be that she was just a grazer. Even now that she is older, she still eats small, frequent meals. Have fun figuring out your baby. As your baby gets older, her feeding pattern will change and you will adjust.

This doesn't mean that you need to watch the clock. Instead, watch your baby's hunger cues. Notice that your breasts feel full. You feel like snuggling with your baby. These are all good reasons to offer your breast to your baby. You may have heard of this philosophy of nursing as "feeding on demand." I have always disliked this phrase and felt that it sounds too harsh, like the mother is being browbeaten to feed the baby at a moment's notice. Rather, I like the phrase "whenever nursing", meaning that you nurse whenever you feel like it or whenever your baby is interested. No pressure, no time constraints. Just doing what feels natural to you and your baby.

Alternate between breasts during each nursing session so you empty both regularly. This avoids looking lopsided. Once you have breastfeeding down, you will be able to feel which breast needs to be emptied next. If it is really hard to tell, you can put a small safety pin on the bra strap of the breast you should start with next time. Or you could have a slip-on bracelet that you move from wrist to wrist, indicating which breast you should start with next time.

What if you plan to pump? When should you do that? If you aren't going to be with your baby and you plan to pump instead, it is important to keep up with a regular schedule. Otherwise, your supply could decrease with less demand. For example, if you are just returning to work, you should pump regularly every three hours. I'll talk more about pumping a little later on, but remember that your baby will always be more efficient than the best pump at stimulating milk production and let down.

If you are giving your baby a bottle for some reason (Grandma is feeding her, you have a dentist appointment, or you and your partner have a date), you need to pump to make up for that missed nursing session. Otherwise, your breasts will get the message that less milk is needed so less milk will be made. This continues to be the rule during your entire breastfeeding relationship.

What Else to Expect

Baby's weight will be back to his birth weight or higher by two weeks. (All babies lose some weight within the first couple of days after birth; this is NORMAL. Your baby's health care provider will watch to make sure it doesn't exceed a comfortable amount.) Your baby goes through natural growth spurts, the first one being around the time he is eight to fourteen days old. During a growth spurt, your baby will feed more often and you may get engorged as your body responds to this increased demand for milk. Be sure to finish on one breast and empty it completely before you offer the second breast. Feeding the baby often and massaging the breast can help to relieve engorgement. If engorgement lasts for more than two days, contact a lactation consultant or your health care provider.

Regardless of whether or not your baby is entering a growth spurt, your will have established your milk supply by 2 weeks postpartum if you breastfeed exclusively. If you feel that your milk supply is not enough for your baby, please contact a lactation consultant for an evaluation. She can offer ways to increase your milk supply, if necessary. Any pain should be resolving at about this time. Again, if not, contact a lactation consultant for help if it hasn't.

Visualize It!

You feel that it's time to nurse your baby. She's only a couple of days old and nursing has been going really well. In fact, you are surprised at how much you are enjoying it! Your baby is just starting to stir in her sleeper. You slowly unwrap her from her blanket, rubbing her belly to arouse her a little. She lets out a sigh, and you smell her sweet breath. As you pick her up, she begins to stretch like a cat. Her hand brushes against your cheek as you sneak a kiss.

You get comfortable in your rocker, prop all of your pillows, and bring your baby closer to you. As you lift your shirt, you begin to massage your breast and express a little colostrum. Large drops of the yellow substance drip from your breast and you know your body is doing exactly what it is supposed to. Your baby latches on, ready for this feeding. She begins to nurse in a rhythmic pattern and it feels very comfortable to you. One of her hands caresses your breast, while she gazes up at you, her mama. You feel relaxed and confident.

Anne Marie's Thoughts

I wanted to breastfeed because I had heard that it was so healthy for the baby. I learned the importance of it and wanted to give my baby the best chance for a healthy immune system.

Before I breastfed, I thought I would have reservations about nursing in public. Then my best friend had a baby and she nursed in public. I got more comfortable with it. This was about a year before I had my baby. When I did have my baby, I got even more comfortable and stopped covering myself with a blanket while nursing. I felt more secure and didn't feel that I needed to hide or apologize for it. I became more confident and didn't care if other people were offended. I wanted to help make it more natural and acceptable for others who wanted to do it.

I didn't go back to work. I used a hand pump to take the edge off in the morning if I needed to. I rented a pump when I went out of town.

I think nursing is so convenient. I went on a hike when my baby was about 11 days old. It was just me, my husband, and my baby on the trail. I just stopped and fed her on the trail when I needed to. I couldn't imagine bringing formula and bottles on the hike and doing all of that.

I never had obstacles or needed a lactation consultant. I had huge support from friends, my doula, and my grandmother. All were big advocates for breastfeeding. I made a decision that I was going to do this and find out how to make it work. I was prepared. When challenges came up, it wasn't a surprise and I dealt with it.

Chapter 6
Positions and Latch:
Getting It Right

· · · · · · · · · · ·

I feel confident nursing my baby in public.

GETTING YOUR BABY IN a good position and latched onto your breast properly is the key to avoiding most breastfeeding problems. Usually if the position and latch are good, everything else falls into place. Having said that, most women feel some discomfort or pain in their nipples at the beginning of a breastfeeding session when their baby latches on. Usually, this feeling goes away in the first few weeks. However, for some women, there can be a bit of discomfort during their entire breastfeeding relationship with their baby. This discomfort should be at the *beginning* of the feeding session, and then subside as the feeding continues. If you are feeling pain the whole time your baby is latched on, take him off and try to relatch him again. If the pain persists, contact your lactation consultant for evaluation.

Before you begin nursing your baby, make sure you are comfortable. Use as many pillows as needed behind your back, under your arms, and on your lap to lift your baby up to the same level as your breast and to support your arms and upper body. There are many products out there to make this easier, such as the Breast Friend and the Boppy. Both are great, but regular old pillows work too. Another method to getting you and your baby comfortable before latching on is to lean back while sitting up so that your baby is laying on you as she nurses.

Have a glass of water, a snack, the telephone, and the remote control next to you. If not, the phone will ring, and you'll realize how thirsty you are as soon as the baby latches on. (By the way, nursing makes you thirsty, so really, have that glass of water ready!)

I bought a small TV tray and set it next to the rocker where I did most of our breastfeeding sessions. This became my "nursing station." Having a small and lightweight table like this was great because I could easily move it whenever I needed to move my nursing station. A friend of mine kept everything she needed in a small basket that she could carry around with her. No matter where she nursed, she had what she needed.

Latch

A good latch is the foundation for breastfeeding. The term "latch" is used to mean how the baby's mouth attaches to the breast. A good latch allows milk to flow easily from your breast to your baby's mouth. It prevents much of the pain associated with breastfeeding and helps to maintain your milk supply. In fact, most of the patients I have seen complained about breastfeeding problems that disappeared once the latch was adjusted.

When latching your baby onto your breast, be sure that his mouth is open VERY wide, like a yawn. Otherwise, he won't get enough breast tissue in his mouth. He should have most of the areola in his mouth, not just the nipple. The milk ducts which need to be compressed to release milk are at the edge and behind the areola. If he is only on the nipple, he won't get any milk and you will get sore nipples.

The baby's chin should be extended into the breast, so she is in the "sniffing position". This allows the nipple to extend to the baby's palate which stimulates sucking. In fact, if your baby is not getting into a good suck pattern, or not sucking at all, try rubbing the roof of her mouth with your clean finger. This will stimulate her sucking reflex and help to organize her suckle. Once she seems to have a good rhythm going, take your finger out of her mouth and quickly replace it with your breast. You will most likely see improvement in her suckling pattern.

When you latch your baby on, allow him to find your nipple, which will result in an asymmetrical latch. Most of the underside of the areola will be in his mouth, rather than the upper side. You bring his head towards your breast, not your breast towards him. If you try to bring your breast to him, you will find yourself in an awkward position that will be difficult to maintain during the entire nursing session. Bringing your baby to your breast also allows for a deeper latch, which will make for better milk flow. You need to bring your baby's head to your breast quickly when he roots, otherwise his mouth will close again. It may feel as though you are smashing your baby into your breast, and you kind of are. But it's a gentle and brief smashing.

Your baby's lips should be flanged out (like fish lips), not tucked in. Often, the bottom lip is the one to get tucked in. Before breaking the latch and taking your baby off of your breast, simply pull his chin down with your finger (or have someone else do it if you can't see his chin). This will often pull the lower lip out and create a better latch. If your baby's lips are tucked in, she will be sucking more on her lips than your breast. This means less milk transfer from breast to tummy, and more sore nipples for mom.

The baby's tongue should curl around the bottom of the nipple, and it should extend out over the gum line. You will be able to see if the tongue is doing this by slightly pulling down on the chin to lower the bottom lip a bit.

You should not hear any slurping sounds. If you do, it means that your baby's mouth has not created a good seal around your nipple and air is getting in. Breathing should be the only sound you hear. You may even hear swallowing, though this is often heard more when your baby is a little older.

To take your baby off the breast you need to break the seal. Don't just pull the baby off. OUCH! Instead, put your finger in the baby's mouth from the side and break the seal between the gums and the breast tissue.

Positions

The position you choose depends on your comfort, the baby's comfort, the baby's age, and sometimes where you are nursing. Below are the descriptions of the four basic positions to nurse in.

Cradle Position
This is the position most people think of when it comes to breastfeeding. The baby's head rests in the crook of the mom's elbow. This is better for older babies, and more difficult for newborns because their neck muscles are not strong enough to keep their head in place. When you use the cradle position

with an older baby, he is actually getting himself into a proper position. You may still have to hold your breast for him to get a good latch, but can usually let go once he is latched on.

Cross Cradle

This is a better position for newborns. You hold your baby's head in position since he doesn't have the neck strength to do it himself yet. If you are nursing on the right breast, your right hand holds the breast, and your left hand holds the bottom of the baby's head. To hold your baby's head, keep the thumb and middle finger under his ears and the palm of your hand across his shoulder blades. Do not keep your hand on his head, otherwise you will push his head into your breast.

In this hold, you control his head so that you can move him to your breast. Even though you are controlling his head, you never want to force your baby to do something he doesn't want to. If he needs to pull away from your breast, he needs to be able to do that. It just might be that he needs to breathe, but your breast tissue is in his way.

"Football" Hold, Underarm Hold or
Clutch Hold

This is a great hold for newborns and for moms who are new at breastfeeding. This hold will allow you to see more of how your baby's mouth and your nipple are coming together, with almost a bird's eye view. If you are feeding on the right breast, hold the baby's head in your right hand (again, with your thumb and middle finger behind his ears, and the palm of your hand against his shoulder blades). Curl his body around your body, keeping his tummy facing your body. You hold your breast with your left hand.

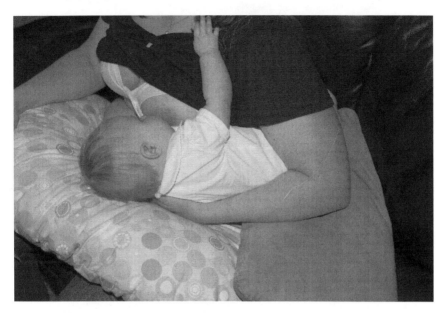

Side Lying

This position allows both mom and baby to lie down while nursing. Great for allowing moms to rest! In fact, both moms and babies can fall asleep in this position, which makes it a great way to nurse at night in bed. Side lying can be harder with a newborn because the baby is unable to latch himself due to weak neck muscles. In the beginning, you may feel like you need 4 hands. That's because you do! It is helpful to have someone help you latch the baby on until you get the hang of it (great job for the other parent). If you are nursing on the left side, your left arm is above your head. You can rest your head on your arm, but do not rest the baby on it. If you rest your baby on your arm, his head will be too flexed for him to latch well or swallow easily. Your baby should be flat on the bed (or wherever you are nursing), just like your body is flat on the bed. Use your right arm to latch the baby on by sliding her close to your body.

Things To Remember About Position

Regardless of which position you choose to nurse in, you want to remember some key things to promote breastfeeding success. Baby's ear, shoulder, and hip should be in one line, so her body isn't twisted. She should be facing your breast as though she were looking right at the nipple. It's harder to swallow if her head is turned to the side.

Mother and baby should be tummy to tummy. This makes for a good position regardless of which one you choose. Wrap your baby's body around yours, so you can get as close as possible.

Hold the baby with your hand on the bottom of her head and top of her shoulders. Your thumb and middle finger should be behind her ears. This allows you to guide and support her head and move it towards your breast when she opens her mouth. Keep her head in the "sniffing" position, meaning that she has a slight tilt upwards as though she is sniffing you. Don't push her head downwards (often this happens if your hand is too high on her head). This puts her neck in a flexed position making it impossible to swallow and it compresses her nose into your breast tissue, making it harder to breathe.

Do not hold your nipple between two fingers. Your fingers will get in the way of your baby's mouth. Instead, form your thumb and forefinger into a "C" or "U" at the edge of the areola. When you compress your breast tissue, make sure you are compressing it in the direction that matches the baby's mouth shape. For example, when we eat a Big Mac, we compress it so the shape of the Big Mac matches the shape of our mouth and fits better. If we were to squeeze it while holding it vertically, it would be perpendicular to the opening of our mouth and never get in.

Bring your baby's body close to you by bringing his buttocks below your opposite breast. This will better allow your baby's mouth to point to the breast being suckled, with the nipple tipped upward. Use pillows if necessary to bring your baby to the height of your breast, and to make these positions more comfortable.

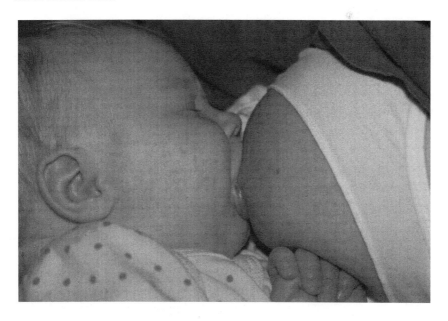

I said it before, but I will say it again: a good position and proper latch are the keys to breastfeeding success, simply because they prevent many of the physical obstacles mom may experience. If you find that you are having trouble with latch and position, please contact a lactation consultant or health care provider for help. The earlier you get help, the quicker you and baby will start the breastfeeding dance and enjoy it.

Visualize It!

It's just before dawn and you are nursing your baby. You decided to sit up for this feeding, instead of lying in bed with her. This is your favorite time to be with your baby: predawn when the house is very quiet and the two of you are alone to snuggle. Both of you always seem to be so alert at this time of morning and you marvel at how you have already fallen into sync with each other. You like to nurse your baby most in the football position because you can see her mouth better. And you like the way it feels to have her body wrapped around yours. As you begin to nurse her, you tickle her lips with your nipple letting her smell the milk, and feel your breast. She instantly acts interested by rooting. She opens her mouth wide, like a yawn, and you bring her head to your breast. Perfect! She latches on without a problem. Her lips are flanged outward and you can feel a tug on your nipple. After a couple of suckles, you feel the warm sensation inside your breasts letting you know that your milk has begun to flow. Now you can hear your baby swallow. The sun starts to shine over the horizon. You stroke your baby's head and count all of her fingers and toes for the hundredth time. You just can't believe she is here! You notice that you start to feel relaxed and a little sleepy. It's the perfect way to start another day.

Julia's Thoughts

I wanted to breastfeed because I knew it was best for me and my baby in terms of health and our connectedness. I always knew that I wanted to breastfeed. That is what breasts are for! I was even more amazed at the miracle of our bodies when I had the personal experience of providing my child all the nutrition that she needed for the first several months of life.

In the first days, weeks and months of my daughter's life some of my sweetest moments were when I was nursing. I felt confident as a mother because I could read her cues and give her what she needed.

Pumping is not the most joyful part of breastfeeding. It is lonely and awkward at times, but I never questioned whether it was worth it. I knew that breast milk was best for my child even if we couldn't have the benefit of the skin-to-skin contact all the time. Sola was such an avid fan of the breast that I never really worried whether she would continue to nurse after I returned to work. I had the opposite problem: she was never really a fan of anything other than the breast.

The first time I put Sola to my breast both of our bodies seemed to know exactly what to do. I didn't stress too much about whether her latch was right or if I was producing enough milk, it just felt right. The rest was history and I know that I am fortunate in this respect.

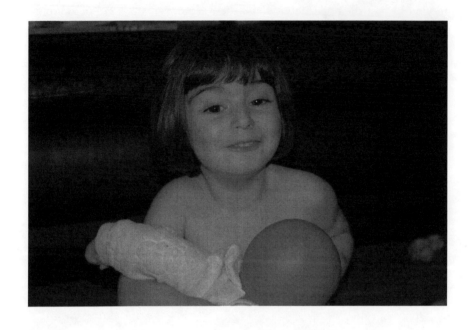

Chapter 7
How Do I Know My Baby Is Getting Enough Milk?

• • • • • • • • • • •

I know how to breastfeed my baby. It is part
of the ancient animal instinct that has allowed
women to nurse their babies for centuries.

IN MY EXPERIENCE, THE number one reason moms stop nursing is their doubt that they have enough milk for their babies. Do you think Mother Nature, God, or whoever you believe came up with breastfeeding, would have created a faulty system? I think not. Of course you can give your baby enough milk for him to thrive and grow! For most women, this is not even an issue. Just put baby to breast often and make sure the latch is a good one.

But you really want to *know* that your baby is getting enough. Something concrete, rather than just an instinct or hunch. Unless there is a sign that your baby needs something more, assume that you have enough milk. It is rare for a mother not to have enough milk for her baby, unless there is a medical issue, or if the breasts are not being stimulated regularly by baby or pump (though baby is always a better stimulator). There are ways to know that your baby is getting the calories and nutrients she needs.

Dirty Diapers

Your baby's dirty diapers are the best indicator that she is getting enough to eat. Your baby should have as many wet diapers as days of life in a twenty-four hour period. For example, if she is three days old, she should have at least three wet diapers. This tells you that your baby is hydrated. After six days, your baby will always have at least 6 wet diapers and at least four poopy diapers. Poopy diapers tell you that your baby is getting enough calories.

Any less and you should call a lactation consultant or your baby's health care provider for help.

Satisfaction

Your baby should appear content after a nursing. Most will even fall asleep. This is a sign that she is satisfied. Just watch that she doesn't fall asleep on the breast if she has nursed for less than ten minutes. This often means that she isn't getting a good milk flow. Try waking her and then relatching her so that she has more areola in her mouth. You can also try compressing your breast tissue while your baby is suckling so that she gets more milk flow.

Back in the day, women were told to nurse on each side for ten minutes (or some other arbitrary number). You don't need to time your baby at the breast. Your baby will take himself off when he is done. However, a feeding should last at least ten minutes of nutritive sucking for most babies. Nutritive sucking is when your baby's jaw moves in a slow rhythmic pattern, his ears wiggle, and he stops to swallow after a few sucks. Often there is a pause while the chin is down during the suck, indicating that his mouth is filling with milk. It is normal for your baby to suck a few times then pause.

Non-nutritive sucking is a more sporadic pattern, maybe five to seven sucks before pausing, with no swallows or constant sucking with no pauses. If your baby is doing this, he won't be getting any milk, as he is not properly compressing the milk ducts. You will also get sore nipples. Take your baby off of the breast and try to relatch, or put slight pressure under is chin to help organize his suck. Another trick to help your baby organize his suck is to put your clean finger in his mouth and stroke the roof of his mouth. This stimulates sucking. Wait until he is sucking in a rhythmic pattern then transfer him from your finger to your breast.

Another reason to not limit your baby's time at each breast is hindmilk. The first bit of milk released during a feeding is foremilk, which is higher in sugar to give your baby a boost of energy. The latter bit of milk is the hindmilk, which is higher in fat. Your baby needs the fat to pack on the weight.

Some babies want to eat more than every three hours. This can be normal and does not mean that your baby is starving. Some babies want to stay at the breast for forty-five minutes. This can also be normal, if you are noticing pauses or swallows, and your baby is indicating that they are satisfied at the breast and getting enough milk. Every baby is unique in their feeding pattern, and all can be variations of normal. As you get to know your baby, you will know his "normal".

Weight Gain

Right after birth, the baby has enough calorie stores built up from when she was inside of you to last her for a bit. All babies lose some weight after birth. This is normal, as long as they don't lose more than 10% of their birth weight. Your baby should be back to her birth weight or more by two weeks of life. If not, or if your baby is consistently losing weight, or has lost more than 10% of her birth weight, contact your baby's health care provider and your lactation consultant to rule out a problem. Do not feel that you need to weigh your baby daily. This will only make you crazy. Assume that your baby is gaining weight, unless she is not satisfied after feedings or she doesn't have enough dirty diapers.

Keep A Record

It's a good idea to write down the number of poops and pees your baby has, as well as when your baby fed. You will be so sleep deprived that you will have no idea how many dirty diapers your baby had that day. Or Dad will change a diaper without you knowing. Just jot this information down on a piece of paper that you keep by the changing table. It doesn't need to be a detailed log!

I once worked with a couple who came to their first postpartum visit with their laptop, which I thought was a little strange. When I asked how often their baby was nursing/peeing/pooping, the dad whipped out the laptop to show me the very impressive spread sheet he had created to chart his baby's bodily functions. I wondered when he had the time to snuggle with his baby if he was working so hard on this spreadsheet. Don't turn this into a project. You just need an easy way to track your baby's daily activity.

Visualize It!

Your baby wakes up and starts to fuss. You change her diaper, but she still seems like she wants something. So you offer her your breast. You just nursed her, maybe an hour ago, but she latches on and nurses beautifully again. In fact, you think she has been nursing more today than usual. She latches on perfectly and is very content to be at the breast. She is always satisfied when she is done, drifting off to sleep peacefully. "Should I be worried that she isn't getting enough milk?" you wonder. Then you remember hearing about growth spurts, when a baby nurses and sleeps more than usual to gain and grow more. Now that you think about it, it is the time she would be growing more. Her clothes are getting smaller and you have started to put her in the next size. She looks fuller and her cheeks are so chubby. You didn't think they could get any chubbier! You aren't worried. You know this is a normal progression. You know that your baby is nursing more often to tell your body to make more milk. It is all just as it should be. Your body and your baby know how to communicate so that you can give her all the nourishment she needs. She is looking at you, very content at the breast. Her lower hand wraps around your torso and gently caresses you. You love that! You feel so proud of her growth and proud that you are making that possible.

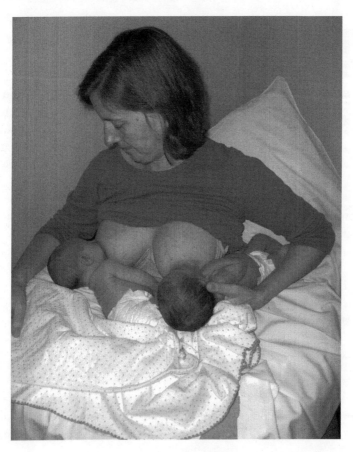

Chapter 8
Obstacles That Can Be Overcome

• • • • • • • • • • •

My breasts are beautiful with a beautiful purpose.

I BELIEVE THAT EVERY woman and baby can breastfeed. I assume that you will have enough milk and your baby will know how to suck. Hopefully, you assume this too! But things do occur that make this a little more challenging at times. *Challenging does not mean impossible.* I had my fair share of breastfeeding challenges when my daughter was born. She was born right at the cut off for "term" babies, meaning that she just missed being called premature. She was big enough to be considered within normal weight for her birth date. However, one ounce less and she would have been considered "small for gestational age". Both of these things meant the possibility that she would have a hard time figuring out how to suck correctly. And to top it off, she was born tongue-tied. This condition can be easily corrected, but it can also mean breastfeeding problems. Ugh! It was an extremely rough start. I had to feed her on my breast while also giving her some expressed breast milk or formula through a tube and syringe every two hours. The tube was taped to my breast and ended at the tip of my nipple so that she could suck on my breast and the tube at the same time. Then I pumped right after each feeding to get my supply up, since her suck was too ineffective to stimulate my breasts adequately. All of this meant that I had forty-five minutes to sleep. You can imagine what a charming person I was with only forty-five minutes of sleep at a time. I felt crazy and couldn't think straight most of the time. I also couldn't do it all alone. But with lots of determination (and tears) and support from my husband, doula, and friends, I nursed my daughter for twenty months. I got engorged; I had sore nipples; I had plugged ducts. And I am a lactation consultant. You would think that I would know how to avoid these issues!

Breastfeeding is a learned behavior and new moms and babies can have a steep learning curve. It's also something that we can't intellectualize. I had lots of education on the subject of lactation, but when it came time to nurse my first daughter, I was too in my head, trying to figure it all out. I was weighing my daughter before and after each feeding. I kept increasing the strength of the pump so that it would get more milk out (really, I just got purple nipples). I was calculating and re-calculating how much formula I had to give her in the first two weeks for her to grow. Feeding my baby had become quite a project. In hindsight, I see that I needed to relax and let our bodies do what they were designed to do. Of course, I needed some good, uninterrupted sleep before I could come to this realization.

As with anything new, it may take a few tries to get it right. But you will get it right with commitment and support! I include information on common obstacles so you at least hear the information once, but hopefully never have to use it.

The information below is intended for educational purposes only. It is not meant to be used to self diagnose or self treat. If you have a concern about yourself or your baby, you should seek medical advice from your lactation consultant, midwife, or doctor.

PHYSICAL ISSUES

Physical issues affect your body. Most of the time, you can avoid or alleviate these issues with frequent feedings and a good latch.

Engorgement
Engorgement occurs when your breasts are too full of milk. Often this happens because of tissue swelling, rather than because of too much milk, but it's still uncomfortable. It can also occur when you miss a nursing session. Your body was expecting you to feed you baby (or pump) and you didn't, so now your breasts are full of milk.

When my second daughter was born, I feared that I would have supply issues. There was no reason for me to worry about this; she was born healthy and ready to nurse. But my fears were based on the difficulties I had with my first daughter and I didn't want a repeat. So, to ensure that *plenty* of milk came in, I pumped a couple of times a day as soon as I got home from the hospital. MISTAKE! I didn't need to pump; my body was on track to do exactly what it was supposed to do. Instead of *trusting* this, I over-pumped and confused my body into thinking I needed enough milk to feed a litter, rather than just one baby. My breasts looked like a science experiment gone awry and felt like they had 500 pound weights hanging from them. I couldn't wear my largest nursing bra (which was a size H!) because my breasts had ballooned to an insane size. Moral of the story: Trust that your milk will come in because your baby is stimulating your body appropriately and don't overdo it with pumping!

The best way to prevent engorgement is to empty your breasts regularly (at least every three hours), and pump when you miss a feeding. If you do get engorged, NURSE! You may need to hand express or pump some milk first because it can be difficult for the baby to latch when your breast is too full and hard. Don't pump too much or your body will think it has to make MORE milk and, thus, more engorgement.

Before nursing, try applying warm, moist heat to your breasts. This can be from showers, hot compresses, or just submerging your breast in a tub of hot water. This will help to release some milk, softening your breasts and making it easier for your baby to latch. Massage before or during feeding to prevent a milk duct from getting plugged. Massaging will break up anything that has accumulated there, while your baby's suckle will keep things moving. After nursing, apply cold compresses to your breasts. This will constrict the blood vessels and ducts to reduce swelling.

Sore Nipples

Often there is pain when the baby first latches. This pain should *not* continue throughout the feeding. If it does, there is usually a reason, so please seek help.

Getting your baby to latch onto your breast correctly is the key to preventing sore nipples (and many other issues). Make sure your baby has as much of the areola in his mouth as possible. If your baby has only latched onto the nipple, you will get sore and your baby won't get much milk. Having your baby in a proper position and varying the positions used can also help. Varying positions rotates your baby's jaw around your areola, which allows for even stimulation of the milk ducts. Continue to feed your baby often.

After feedings, express and rub some milk onto your nipple and areola to aid in healing the skin, then allow to air dry. Breast milk has antibiotic properties, which aid in healing and preventing infection. When you are

—

done nursing, break the suction with your finger before pulling baby off your nipple. Just pulling your baby off will definitely cause pain!

Avoid soaps, alcohol or creams on your nipples. These can dry or irritate the skin. One exception is Lanolin, which is sold under a few different brand names. Lanolin is a soothing ointment made from wool extract, so do not use it if you have a wool allergy. If you do have a wool allergy, use Soothies. These are gel-like pads made of about 98% water and can be found in most drugstores. Avoid leaving wet nursing pads on for long periods of time. This can irritate the skin and cause a yeast infection in this area. Apply Lanolin and Soothies after each feeding. These products offer lots of relief and can be found at most drugstores. Lanolin will not affect your baby, so there is no reason to clean your nipple before feedings.

If you develop sore nipples, feed your baby when she shows early signs of hunger rather than waiting until she is very hungry. If too hungry, your baby will act like a barracuda on your nipple. Feed more often for less time to reduce the irritation. Feed on the less sore side first. When your baby is most hungry she will have a stronger suck which could be more painful.

If your pain is severe or there is a lot of broken down skin, use a nipple shield or pump for twenty-four hours (rather than nurse) and feed expressed milk with a bottle, cup, or spoon to give your nipples a little time off to heal. If the soreness persists for more than three days or the nipple becomes cracked or blistered, see a lactation consultant or your health care provider to rule out an infection and to troubleshoot problems with the latch.

Plugged Ducts

Plugged ducts occur when a milk duct becomes plugged and the milk is unable to drain from it. It is usually caused by a longer space of time between feedings (ie: you skipped a usual feeding or your baby starts to sleep during the night). You may feel a tender lump in your breast or it may feel warm to the touch.

You could experience a plugged duct at any time during your breastfeeding relationship with your baby. I had a plugged duct when my daughter was a couple of months old, a year old, and 18 months old, and probably at times in between. To prevent plugged ducts, change nursing positions often so that all of your milk ducts are drained evenly. Don't wear clothes or bras that are too tight. This causes pressure against the milk ducts, making it harder for the milk to flow through them. Make sure the straps of your baby carrier and diaper bag do not put pressure on your breasts.

To resolve a duct that is already plugged, apply moist heat before nursing. Massage the plugged area during nursing. The massage breaks down whatever is plugging the duct. Your baby will pull it out while nursing, clearing the blocked duct. A good way to massage the area is to put the bottom end of an electric toothbrush, such as a Sonicare, on the clogged duct. (I wonder if this company has any idea their product is used for this!) You can also manually massage the area. I think the electronic toothbrush works faster to get the job done, but it does distract the baby from nursing. If it is awkward to massage and nurse, massage right before your baby latches on. Call your health care provider or lactation consultant if the lump or pain doesn't go away in two days.

Mastitis

Mastitis is an infection of the breast tissue. Even though the infection is only in your breast, you feel it all over. Mastitis can really knock you down, so get help at home if you can. Since it isn't contagious, those helping you don't need to worry that they will get sick also. Whether you have a friend or family member come over, or you hire a postpartum doula, you will appreciate someone making you lunch and taking care of the baby.

Symptoms of mastitis include:

- red area on your breast
- skin is hot to touch
- fever
- general malaise
- a feeling that you have the flu.

The best way to prevent mastitis is to prevent plugged ducts and sore/cracked nipples. A breakdown in your skin is an open doorway for bacteria to get inside your body and cause an infection. Keep the area as clean as possible. Change nursing pads, or better yet, don't use them while you have an open sore or crack in your skin. Wash your hands before touching your breasts.

If mastitis develops, you will need to contact your health care provider to prescribe antibiotics. It is also important that you rest and drink plenty of fluids. Continue to breastfeed! Yes, it may hurt, but it is important to continue nursing so your milk supply stays up. Even with diligence, some women do experience a drop in their supply in the breast that was infected. If you persevere and continue to breastfeed, the drop will be less than if you stopped nursing while sick.

Thrush

Thrush is a yeast infection in the breast and nipple area. Your symptoms are a pink and tender nipple, which may itch, or flaky skin. Your breast may be swollen. You may also have shooting pains in your breast during and after nursing.

It can also be in the baby's mouth. Your baby's symptoms are a red, irritated diaper rash, or a white patch in the mouth that can't be wiped away. (If the white patch can be wiped away, it's just milk residue.) If the sores in your baby's mouth are very sore, it may be uncomfortable for her to nurse.

Thrush can take up to two weeks to completely resolve, which can seem like an eternity. As with any infection, good hand washing is key in prevention. It also keeps yeast from spreading from breast to genital area or vice versa. Wash hands before and after feedings, diaper changes, and visits to the bathroom. Other ways to prevent yeast infections are to avoid sugar (yeast thrives on sugar) and antibiotics, if possible (antibiotics kill everything, even the good flora in your body that protects you from this type of infection). Do not leave wet nursing pads on for long periods of time; change them often.

While treating a yeast infection, wash bras in very hot water and change them often. Do not wear the same bra two days in a row unless it has been washed. Sterilize bottles and pacifiers after each use. A vinegar wash (just vinegar diluted with water) on your nipple will change the pH of your skin enough to hinder the yeast from increasing. Make sure you rinse the area before you nurse, as babies don't really like the smell or taste of vinegar.

Acidophilus (good bacteria found in our guts and in yogurt) taken in the form of capsules, liquid, or plain, organic yogurt can give your body an extra boost in the fight against yeast infections. If you are taking antibiotics, take the acidophilus an hour after your medication. You can buy powdered acidophilus to use on your breasts. Mix the powder with water to make a paste and apply to your nipples. Powdered acidophilus made especially for babies is available at health food or vitamin stores. You can apply it to the white patches in your baby's mouth. If the infection persists, see your health care provider, as you may need a prescription for an antifungal medication. You should also see your baby's provider, as your baby will most likely need medication for the thrush in her mouth and her diaper rash. Both of you will need to be treated, even if your baby has no symptoms. Otherwise, you will continue to pass the infection to each other.

Mom's illness
If you are sick with the cold or flu, you won't pass it to you baby through your milk (though you want to avoid coughing on your baby and wash your hands). In fact, you will pass antibodies against the illness through your milk, which strengthens your baby's immune system. Nursing your baby while you are sick actually protects her from getting ill, too. You may need to wear a mask while you nurse to prevent spreading the virus while breathing on your baby.

Many medications are safe to take while breastfeeding. However, you should always check with a lactation consultant or your baby's pediatrician before taking any medications while nursing.

Inverted Nipples
About one in three women have inverted nipples, but they may evert by the end of pregnancy. If you put your thumb and forefinger at the borders of your areola and press them toward the chest wall and your nipple goes inward, it is inverted. If this is the case, your baby may have difficulty latching at first, though with time, your baby may draw your nipple out. A nipple shield can help with this also. It is a good idea to meet with a lactation consultant before your baby is born, so she can help you latch your baby on from day one.

EMOTIONAL ISSUES

As in life, many obstacles women encounter while nursing are more emotional than physical in nature. How do we feel about breastfeeding our baby in public or as a toddler or when we want more freedom? These can be harder to treat than the physical symptoms. Talking these out with your partner or other nursing moms can help gain some perspective.

Lack of confidence
Many new parents fear that they aren't doing this right, or that their baby is not getting enough to eat. Babies have been surviving on mother's milk for centuries. KNOW that your body is producing enough milk!

Before you give birth, let your partner and your family and friends know how important breastfeeding is to you. Surround yourself with cheerleaders who believe in you and what you are doing for you and your baby.

Embarrassed to feed in public

If you had to eat in public, you would, right? Your baby needs to eat too and that's what breasts are for! Our sex-crazed culture has made breasts sexual and tried to make women feel embarrassed by them. I hope it hasn't done this to you. More and more places are offering areas for nursing moms and there are many fashionable blankets or ponchos available now to add flair to your discretion. However, keep in mind that even without covering up, most women are showing less breast tissue while nursing than they would show if wearing a simple low-cut shirt. And of course, we all feel a little less embarrassed when we have a supportive person with us. Hopefully, you will feel so confident that you will use the opportunity of someone's stare or negative comment to educate them on the benefits and importance of breastfeeding!

I have never been embarrassed to nurse in public. I do not cover up, but I practice discretion. I am also lucky that I live in an area that is very pro-breastfeeding, so it is common to see women nursing in public places. I have also surrounded myself with other nursing moms, so we nurse together when in public. Strength in numbers.

Only once in my four years of nursing have I gotten any hassle while in public. I was at a museum in Florida. I sat on a bench, facing a wall, away from the crowd and nursed my daughter. How much more discreet could I be? Apparently, a lot more.

A female security guard in her 60's approached me and our exchange went like this:

Her: Are you nursing your baby?

Me: (smiling sweetly) Yes, I am.

Her: Come on, I'll show you the back room. (At this point she walks away, just *assuming* I would follow her.)

Me: Oh, thanks, but it doesn't bother me to stay here.

Her: It doesn't bother me either, but it'll bother someone. Let's go.

I stood up, with my baby in my arms, and yelled at the top of my lungs, "I have the right to remain right here and nurse my baby, dammit!"

Ok, so I didn't really say that. I was tired from a long day of traveling. My daughter had worn me out with many bouts of crying and I felt deflated from the day before this security guard even approached me. I didn't have the fight in me, so I went to the back room. My husband found me there 20 minutes later, after a frantic search. When he asked why I was in the back room, I almost broke into tears because I hadn't stood up for myself and my baby. He just put his arm around me and said that I was still a good mom and lactation advocate no matter what I did or didn't say to that security guard. I'm planning another trip to Florida and I'm tempted to go back to that museum just so I can nurse RIGHT IN FRONT OF THAT SECURITY GUARD. I'm ready this time!

State Law
There are many state laws which exempt breastfeeding from any indecent exposure laws and encourage employers to set up breastfeeding stations at work. It is a good idea to know what the law is in your state. In case anyone asks you to stop breastfeeding because of "indecency," you can quickly respond with confidence that you are in the right. You can find out the laws in your state from the National Conference of State Legislatures at http://www.ncsl. org/programs/health/breast50.htm#w

Diet
Women feel they need to give up certain foods, thanks to a bunch of myths out there such as broccoli, garlic and spicy foods upset babies' tummies. There has never been any scientific evidence that certain foods explicitly affect babies negatively. It is on a baby-by-baby basis. If you think that a food is bothering your baby, delete it from your diet for two weeks, and then reintroduce it. If your baby seems to be less gassy, fussy, or rashy when you eliminated that food, then maybe it was the food. Avoid it until you wean.

Lack of support from partner/family
Research has shown that mothers stop breastfeeding sooner when there is no support, especially if family members did not breastfeed. Breastfeeding can be hard, and moms need to have support to remember why they are doing this! There may be other factors in your personal history that make breastfeeding

more difficult such as breast surgery or a history of sexual assault. Go to your support when you need it.

Visualize It!

You are out for lunch with your baby and a girlfriend. Your baby is asleep most of the time while you and your girlfriend eat and catch up with each other. But now he is awake and wants lunch too! You get him out of his stroller and place him on your lap. This is the first time you nurse in public. You are nervous, but confident. Your friend has an older child she nursed, so she encourages you to nurse in public. The restaurant isn't full, but there are a few people there. You are ready.

You position your baby across your lap and place a blanket over your shoulder and breast. With one hand you unclasp your bra and lift your shirt. You are able to see your baby's head under the blanket so you get him latched on. It takes a couple of tries because you feel awkward with the blanket and being in public. But the latch is good and your baby nurses well. Nobody is watching you. Your friend congratulates you on your first public nursing and you two continue your conversation. After a minute or two, you forget that you are nursing your baby in public and the awkward feeling passes. When your baby finishes nursing, you are able to lower your shirt and remove the blanket easily and discreetly. You are proud of yourself! Nursing in public only gets easier and easier after this.

Susan's Thoughts

With my first born, I felt very strongly about natural childbirth. I felt that my body was made to do this and the baby was made to do this. The birth was good; I did it my way and had a natural birth. So I was really surprised when I had a hard time breastfeeding because the birth was so empowering and so awesome. I thought breastfeeding would be a snap. I didn't realize that breastfeeding could be hard and that it was a learning process. Fortunately, I have a pediatrician that is very pro-breastfeeding and she held my hand through the whole thing. My baby had a bad latch, so I had every problem you could imagine. I just couldn't produce enough. My mom had the same problem. I just thought, what is wrong with me? Why can't I do this? So we went to formula after a month, but I still comfort nursed him. I really wanted him to have some of that connection. I did that for about 4 months.

With baby #2, I was warned that I might have the same problems again.

My doula said, "We know that there is a problem here, so we are going to really address that." And she spent all of her time as a doula working with me and breastfeeding. My second baby's latch is definitely different; she acts like she has done this before. But I still didn't produce enough. I pumped whenever I could, but still couldn't get enough. So my doula recommended I try Domperidone.* Once I started taking this, I had a huge difference in milk supply. I'm actually able to nurse my baby now. I still supplement at night, but that is all. My insurance doesn't pay for it and it's really expensive. But it's so worth it to me to be able to feed her and I'm so glad I found it. I feel like we're a team. I'm not even sure I know how to describe the bond, but it's very different than the bond with my first child. Because my first child could take a bottle, I was able to leave him with other people more easily. And even though it didn't feel so right to me, I left him with others at a younger age. I shared him more. With my second baby, it's like I can't. I don't like other people to give her a bottle.

I really believe in breastfeeding, it's just the way it's supposed to be. It's the most perfect relationship in nature; the way mom and baby go together. Why mess with it if you don't have to? It's incredible when you think about how your body produces milk and just knows what you're baby needs. It's wild!

My neighbor has a baby who is exclusively breastfed and he is just HUGE. Whenever I see him, I just think, "Way to go, Mom! Woohoo!" She must be so proud.

Why did I try so hard to continue nursing my first child? I don't know. It just seemed like something I had to do. Birth was this natural process, I just thought breastfeeding would be the same way. Because I had such a hard time the first time around, I envied women who can just nurse. But now, I do it almost defiantly.

*Domperidone is a prescription medication that can increase milk supply, but it is not FDA approved in the United States. Reglan is a medication that is approved and available in the US, which has an off-label use to increase milk supply. (Both drugs are more commonly used for gastrointestinal issues.) However, domperidone has fewer side effects than Reglan, such as anxiety and depression. It can be difficult to find a health care provider willing to prescribe domperidone, and even harder to find a pharmacy that carries it. If you do have a prescription for this drug, take it to a compounding pharmacy so they can make the formula there. Either drug should only be used after a mother has tried other methods to increase her milk supply. More information on galactogogues (medications or herbs that increase milk supplt) can be found in Appendix 3.

Chapter 9
Breastfeeding, Sex, and Birth Control

• • • • • • • • • • •

I trust my body to nourish my baby.

LET'S TALK ABOUT SEX. After all, it's what got you into this situation. Some of you may be thinking, "What sex?" You may not be interested in it now, but one day you will be. I promise. And if you forget all about it, I'm sure your partner will remind you that you used to enjoy partaking in the act.

It's understandable and normal for sex to be the last thing on your mind after you have a baby. This is the case for many women. You are tired, sore, and you may feel that your body is no longer your own. Everyone wants a piece of you emotionally and physically.

Sexuality

The changes in your hormones during pregnancy and breastfeeding can affect your sexuality. You may experience a decrease in your sex drive. (Of course, this can also be due to lack of sleep.) You may have noticed less lubrication during intercourse. The positions you once enjoyed regularly may no longer be an option. To deal with these issues, make sure you are interested in sex. Women often need our minds to be engaged in sex first and then our bodies will follow. And even if you aren't interested, you might want to do it anyway. Most of us "get into the mood" once we start. Feel free to use lubrication as needed and make it a part of foreplay. Astroglide and Slippery Stuff are good ones to try. Experiment with new positions.

While you are nursing, you may experience a surprise with your orgasm. As mentioned before, oxytocin is released during an orgasm. Remember, this

67

is the hormone that causes the letdown reflex or milk ejection. Thus, milk may leak during lovemaking. It may even spray out. This can be quite unexpected for you and your partner. Try to have fun with it and use your sense of humor to get through this. If it really bothers either of you, nurse your baby before you have sex, or just wear a bra to keep the milk from getting all over you.

If you really aren't in the mood for intercourse, don't do it. Try other ways to express your love and desire for intimacy. Cuddling, kissing, showering with each other, dinner without the baby, and a long walk while holding hands are just some examples of ways to feel close without having sex. Most of all, try to keep a positive attitude about rediscovering your body and what feels good in light of your physical and emotional changes. If you are having physical pain during intercourse, see your health care provider for an evaluation.

Lactational Amenorrhea Method (LAM)

Breastfeeding exclusively and "whenever" (or "on demand") can keep estrogen levels low enough that a new mom doesn't ovulate or get her period for several months. In fact, it isn't unusual for some women to go a year or longer without periods while they are nursing.

In past centuries, this was a way for families to space their children. LAM can be used as a natural birth control method if the following criteria are met:

- Mom's period has not started yet. Ovulation occurs before menstruation, so if you have a period, there is a big chance you are ovulating.

- The baby is breastfed around the clock. No supplements of any kind or pacifiers are given.

- The baby is less than 6 months old.

When LAM is used correctly, it is 98% effective as a means of birth control, as long as breastfeeding has been well established. (10) If the above criteria are not met, there is a risk of pregnancy without another type of birth control. If you aren't nursing your baby exclusively and whenever she asks, if you have developed a strict feeding schedule, or if you give your baby a pacifier or bottles, this method cannot be relied on to prevent pregnancy. Your estrogen and progesterone levels may elevate enough to allow ovulation to occur because you aren't breastfeeding enough to suppress them. This means pregnancy is a possibility. If the thought of having another baby in nine months or so sends chills up your spine, use another birth control method! However, if you stick to the above rules, LAM can be a valid option for birth control.

Other Birth Control Options

It may seem crazy now, but you will want to have sex one day, probably before your kids are in college. When that time comes, be prepared! When choosing a birth control method to use while breastfeeding, there are a few things to consider. Methods that contain estrogen are not recommended while nursing. Estrogen can greatly diminish your milk supply. You also want to think about what birth control you used in the past and how your body responded to it. Think about how birth control will fit into your daily life. Will you remember to take it every day? Do you mind having to think about it before sex every time? Determine how many years you want between your pregnancies, or even if you want more babies. Do you want to have another baby sooner than later? Knowing the answers to these questions will help you determine which birth control method is right for you.

The birth control methods that contain estrogen include: Combination Oral Contraceptives (most pills), Nuva Ring, and Ortho Evra Patch. If you do choose to use one of these methods, it is recommended that you wait until your baby is at least 6 months old and well established on solid foods.

That leaves birth control methods that contain progestin only (the synthetic version of progesterone) or no hormones at all. There is even some controversy that progestin-only birth control can affect milk supply, though not as much as estrogen-containing methods. There have been studies which show no decrease in milk supply and studies which show a small amount. Dr. Jack Newman, of the Newman Breastfeeding Clinic and Institute in Toronto, recommends that you try the progestin-only pill (the "mini pill") for one month to determine if your milk supply is affected. That way, if you find a significant drop, you can discontinue the pill and work towards increasing your supply again. If you find no change in supply, you are probably safe to use a progestin-only method. (The other progestin-only methods are not easily discontinued, which is why it is suggested to try the mini pill first.)

It is best to wait until about six to eight weeks postpartum to start a progestin-only birth control method. (10) If you feel that your baby is not nursing well, not gaining weight, or you think there has been a change in your milk supply, discontinue the birth control and see if things improve. Consult with a lactation consultant or your baby's health care provider if you are concerned.

Birth control methods that can be used while breastfeeding are described below. As with any medication, talk to your health care provider about which one is best for you.

Progestin Only Pills ("The Mini Pill")

The mini pill is swallowed every day *at the same time*. If you take your pill more than three hours later than the usual time, you run the risk of pregnancy. Three hours can be enough time for the level of synthetic hormones to drop, allowing your own hormones to work again. Ovulation is more likely to occur when this happens. The "mini pill" isn't a good choice if you have an erratic schedule. The most common side effect is irregular bleeding.

DepoProvera Shot

DepoProvera contains progestin only and is given to you at the clinic every twelve weeks by a shot in the arm or buttocks. The common side effects of this are irregular bleeding, weight gain, and an increased risk of osteoporosis. Because of the risk of osteoporosis, it is recommended to take a calcium supplement daily and participate in weight bearing exercises while on DeprProvera. (Your baby is a great weight!) If you have a strong family or personal history of depression, this is not a good choice for you, as it can cause or worsen depression.

Intrauterine Device (IUD)

An IUD is inserted into your uterus through the vagina and cervix while you are at the clinic. If you have had a vaginal delivery, it can be inserted very easily with minimal discomfort. If you have not had a vaginal delivery, you will experience some cramping during insertion. It is recommended to take ibuprofen before insertion, as well as to use a heating pad to ease the cramps. Most people are able to continue with their usual activities with no problems after the IUD is inserted.

There are two types of IUDs and both can be used while nursing. The first is the Mirena, which contains progestin and can be left in the uterus for five years. The most common side effect is irregular bleeding, which can mean anything from spotting every day to no period at all.

The other type of IUD is the Paragard, which contains copper and no hormones. The copper acts as a spermicide. It can be left in place in the uterus for up to ten years. Common side effects are heavy bleeding and cramping. Both IUDs work by impeding the movement of sperm and egg, affecting the lining of your uterus, and stopping fertilization from occurring. IUDs are not abortifacients, which means they do not cause the demise of a fertilized egg.

Because the Paragard has no hormones, it does not affect your cycles, so you will have your period whenever you normally have it. Once the Paragard is removed, your fertility is immediately resumed. Because the Mirena contains progestin, it thins the lining of your uterus, which is one of the ways it affects your periods. Once the Mirena is removed, it may take a few months for your periods to return back to normal, allowing you to get pregnant.

Implanon

Implanon is a single rod containing progestin that is inserted into the upper part of your arm. It's the size of a match stick and is inserted in a way similar to a getting a shot. It slowly releases the hormone over a three year period. It can only be inserted and removed in a clinic. The most common side effect is irregular bleeding, which can mean anything from spotting every day to no period at all.

Non- Hormonal Birth Control Methods

Non-hormonal birth control methods do not affect your hormones or milk supply. These include the diaphragm, male and female condom, spermicidal foam/jelly, and the sponge. The risk of pregnancy is slightly higher with non-hormonal methods because your body is still able to ovulate, making you fertile. There is more user error (hey, we're all human) because you have to think about birth control before you have sex, often while in the heat of the moment.

The withdrawal method (when the man withdraws his penis before he has an orgasm, also known as the "pullout" method) is NOT a birth control method. Just ask my best friend. She had two kids using this method of birth control. There are sperm present in the man's pre-ejaculate, which means he can drop off baby-producing sperm *before* he has an orgasm. Don't rely on this to prevent pregnancy.

Sterilization

Sterilization means that you have altered your body surgically so that pregnancy is not possible. For women, this is called a tubal ligation, which is a procedure in which the fallopian tubes are severed, sealed, or pinched shut to prevent fertilization. The egg is not able to descend and meet the sperm. Vasectomy is the sterilization procedure for men. During a vasectomy, the vas deferens are sealed, which prevents sperm from being ejaculated. These two procedures should only be considered for people who do not desire any more pregnancies.

None of the methods described above, hormonal or not, protect you from sexually transmitted diseases, except condoms.

Visualize It!

You and your baby enjoy a day together. The weather is perfect: warm and sunny, but not too hot. You decide to spend the day outside at the beach (or you can choose another outdoor place that brings you peace.) You carry your baby in a sling and it feels very comfortable to you. Your body feels strong after the birth and you walk with him easily. He is snuggling against your chest, not really asleep, but very calm. The seagulls are flying overhead, calling out to each other. You walk in time with the crash of the waves against the shore. There is nobody around but you and your baby.

Now your baby starts to root towards your breast, so you decide to stop and nurse him. You find a clear spot where you can sit comfortably in the dry sand. You remove your baby from the sling and position him to your breast. There is nobody around, so you don't feel timid to lift your shirt. Your baby latches easily to your breast and begins to nurse. You smile down at him and he looks right at you. His legs wrap around your body, his hand reaches up to your cheek. You kiss all 5 of his fingers. The wind gently blows his wisps of hair. You take a mental picture of this moment. Then you close your eyes and lift your face to the sun. You feel very relaxed as your baby nurses and the waves almost hypnotize you. A perfect day, indeed.

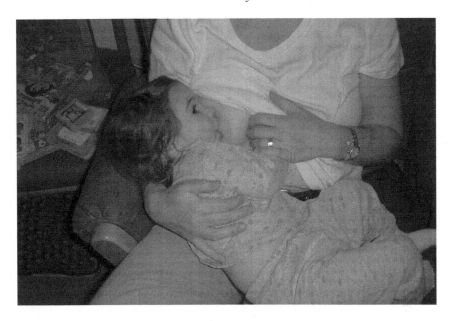

Chapter 10
Pumping While Away From Baby

••••••••••••

I am impressed by my body's effortless
production of milk for my baby.

MANY MOMS WORRY THAT they will have to stop breastfeeding when they go
back to work. Not so! Expressing breast milk (pumping) can enable moms to
work and still provide enough breast milk for their babies, with no need to
supplement with formula. However, it does take commitment from you.

Pumping can bring about some conflicting feelings. On the one hand, it is
great that there is a way for you to continue giving your baby breast milk, even
if you are separated; what a step for the modern woman! But pumping can
also feel like a burden: carrying the pump around, taking time out to pump
multiple times a day, cleaning the equipment more than once. I pumped
religiously for nine months and was so thankful for this option, but there
were many days when I hated it! At times, it felt like something I had to do,
rather than something I wanted to do. I stayed motivated by remembering
that this was the best thing I could do for my baby while away from her. If
you feel weighed down by pumping, try to remember the big picture. You
are providing your baby with optimal nutrition. This is a gift that only you
can give.

What to Think About Before You Get to Work

I recommend working moms invest in a good electric double pump.
I know electric pumps are more expensive, but when it comes to pumps,
you often get what you pay for. An electric double pump is more effective
at expressing more milk in less time. Battery operated pumps or manual

pumps don't have enough power for most people. If you are pumping a lot, you really need to have the most power you can get. If you aren't going back to work or school and only plan to pump occasionally, you may not need to invest in an electric pump. A less powerful, less expensive pump (such as a manual/hand pump) may be all that you need for the occasional separation from your baby.

Use a double pump that expresses milk from both breasts at the same time. Pumping both breasts at the same time increases your prolactin levels even more, thus you will get more milk. This is possible with most electric pumps. It also saves you time because you pump both breasts in the time you would have to pump one with a single pump. The time-saving factor might be really important to you if you have limited time at work to do this.

Before your first day back at work, pump while still at home to collect a reserve of milk in your freezer. I recommend pumping and storing milk at least one month prior to your first day back. You may need to start earlier than that if you find that you don't pump out much milk when you are nursing during the day too. Just be sure that you have a supply in the freezer beforehand. This way you won't feel pressure to "keep up" with your baby's appetite, and you will have a sense of how much milk you are able to pump out. While pumping for my first daughter, I thought I had lots of milk in the freezer; I wasn't worried about running out. Besides, I only worked three days a week. I would pump while at work *and* on the days I was home with my daughter to keep up a surplus of milk. However, my body didn't respond to the pump as well as it did to my daughter, and I didn't pump out tons of milk like I thought I would. After a couple of months back at work, my freezer looked pretty empty and I was worried I wouldn't be able to give her enough milk while I was gone. In the end, I did manage to keep enough milk in storage, but I had to play "catch up" for a while by pumping more on the days I was home with her.

Before you even go back to work, give your baby a practice bottle feeding. Then give at least a small amount in a bottle every day so your baby remembers how to drink from a bottle. When I was a new lactation consultant, I worked with a couple who was very worried about their baby refusing a bottle when the mom went back to work. Their friends' baby had refused a bottle when his mom returned to work and he caused a lot of stress for them all. I assured them that most babies have no problems taking a bottle when offered. How wrong I was! I have met many babies who have not wanted a bottle after nursing for a while, including both of mine. Eventually mine did take a bottle, but not without some sweat on my part. So give your baby some bottle practice time, if needed. And remember, if you give a full feeding from a bottle, pump to make up for that feeding.

Try to have your first day back at work be a Thursday or Friday. You just have to get through one or two days at work before you have a break. You are home for two days over the weekend, which is plenty of time to remind you and your baby that you may go away, but you always come back. It can be overwhelming to leave your baby for the whole week after spending three or four months or longer at home with her. Not to mention you have to throw yourself back into "work mode", and pump regularly all at the same time. You will be juggling your personal and professional lives in a whole new way.

Be sure to carry a photo of your baby with you when you pump at work. Look at a photo of your baby while pumping to initiate the let down. Seeing your baby creates an emotional response that affects your hormones too. Don't forget to have a cooler bag and ice pack with you at work. You will need these to carry your expressed milk home during your commute.

Before you go back to work, think about the logistics of pumping there. You will need a private place where you can relax and pump, and that has a sink for washing pump materials and a refrigerator to store expressed milk. A bathroom stall doesn't count as a private place! You may need to ask your co-workers or boss to help you find an appropriate place to pump, where you can feel relaxed.

I knew a woman who worked full time and pumped at work every day. She did not have an office, but worked in a cubicle, so she would have to walk down the hall and borrow someone else's office to pump. Her day was packed with meetings and conference calls. She would often be so busy that she would miss a pumping. After a few days of this pattern, her milk supply started to decrease. When she called me, she was in a panic that she would have to wean before she intended. Luckily, I was able to offer some suggestions to increase her supply (it did), and I was able to strategize with her about how she could better plan more pumping sessions in her day. She devised a plan where she scheduled "meetings" in her calendar so that others would know that she was unavailable. She was able to work her pumping sessions into the coworker's schedule whose office she borrowed. That way she always knew it would be available for her. And she rented a hospital grade pump for maximum power while working towards increasing her supply again. Eventually things worked out and she was able to continue pumping and providing her baby with breast milk.

At Work

Obviously, while you are at work or school, you aren't with your baby. So you bring out the pump. When you pump, you are really stimulating your breasts (demand) so that they know to make milk even though you aren't with your baby. Otherwise, what will happen? Your milk supply will decrease. Good, you've been paying attention!

Because you still require the same amount of milk production, you need to stimulate your breasts the same number of times you would if you were with your baby. You still need to pump or breastfeed at least eight times in a twenty-four hour period or at least every three hours. If you work a nine hour day, you are probably going to pump at least three times while there.

Pump both breasts for ten to fifteen minutes. Consider commute time to your "pumping station" if you have a limited amount of time for your break. Will you have to walk across the room, or across campus to get there?

Talk to your boss about what you need to make pumping more successful for you at work. Many companies are realizing that it is cost effective to support working moms who are breastfeeding. Their employees are happier and take fewer days off to care for sick babies. Healthier babies use fewer health care dollars, which benefits the company's bottom line, too.

If you need to persuade your employer to offer support, here are some other things to point out. All of these benefit the employer when their working mothers can securely pump breast milk at work.

- Moms want to keep working! There is reduced staff turnover and loss of skilled workers after the birth of a child, if the mother is able to pump at work. It's expensive to train new employees.

- Healthier babies mean moms are able to go to work. There is less sick time/personal leave for breastfeeding women and their partners because their infants are more resistant to illness.

- Lower health care costs are associated with healthier, breastfed infants.

- Happy moms = happy employees. This translates to an overall higher job productivity, employee satisfaction and morale.

- Women will want to work at a company that supports them and their families.

Storage of Expressed Breast Milk

Human milk can spoil over time just like any other milk product. You want to know how long it has been out and where it was stored so that you can give your baby the freshest milk available. And, of course, always store your milk in a clean container. Choose a container that is glass or hard plastic, with a tight fitting top. Plastic bottles should be bisphenol (BPA) free. This chemical, found in many plastic products, has been found to be toxic to humans. Disposable bottles and those with bag liners are not recommended as they can cause more contamination and leak.

Wash your bottles with hot, soapy water before you use. Rinse them well and allow them to air dry. Write the date on the bottle so you know when it needs to be used. If you are sending your baby to daycare, make sure the bottles are clearly marked with the date, time, and baby's name.

Once you have pumped your milk, it is good for six to eight hours at room temperature. If you choose to freeze it, do so before the eight hours are up and chill it in the refrigerator before putting it in the freezer. Actually, the milk you have pumped will have fewer bacteria in it at the end of this time due to the protective quality of breast milk. It is literally eating away the bacteria. However, longer than this is too much time, and the enzymes of the milk will start to break down, allowing some bacterial growth. According to the Center for Disease Control and Prevention, pumped milk can be kept in the refrigerator for up to five days. It can be kept three to six months in a freezer that has a separate door from the refrigerator and six to twelve months in a deep freezer. (11)

You can pump your milk into bottles that fit directly onto the pump, or in plastic bags that are designed to fit on the pump. If you choose to use the bags, you can seal them, write the date and time on the bag and put them in the freezer as is. The one issue with doing this is that you may end up thawing more milk than you need (if the bag has a lot of milk in it) and it will be wasted. My heart would break whenever I wasted pumped milk because it took so much work to get it!

An easier, and less wasteful way to store milk is to put it in a covered ice cube container, then stick it in the freezer. They even sell containers with sealable tops just for this purpose. The night before you need the milk, you can take out the number of cubes you need for the next day. It's helpful to know how much milk each cube holds. I used this method for storing my milk. I knew that eight cubes in my ice tray equaled five ounces. Figure this out using water in the trays before you start storing your milk in them. Put the cubes in the bottle in the refrigerator the night before so they start to thaw. This allows you to thaw only the amount you need each day. And it's in the bottle, ready to go.

Once frozen milk has been thawed it should be used within twenty-four hours. Never refreeze thawed milk. Never microwave milk to heat it up. This can create hot spots that can burn your baby. It also breaks down the protein and diminishes the antibacterial, antiviral, and immune properties of the milk. Warm the milk with a bottle warmer, or by placing the bottle in a cup of hot water.

Keep your pump supplies clean. If you have access to a refrigerator, you can keep your supplies there in between pumping and wash them once a day. If you can't keep them in a refrigerator, wash them after each use, so they are clean and ready to go for the next pump session. This gives them time to air dry by the time you need them. It also keeps you organized if you are pumping at work during a short break. Sterilize your materials once a week. You can do this by boiling them the old fashioned way, or you can buy special bags that will do the job in the microwave by adding water.

It isn't recommended to share any pump materials that touch your skin or the milk. This can lead to cross contamination. You can share the motor part of the pump, but each person should get her own set of anything that touches her body.

Getting Support While Pumping

Pumping can be freeing in the sense that you can leave your baby and know she will still receive your milk while you are gone. It can also be grueling. Some women don't mind it, but others feel silly hooking a pump to their breasts at first. Some feel burdened with the schedule while they are at work. Others appreciate the chance for a break to focus on their baby. However you feel about pumping, it can be hard to continue if you don't have the support of those at work, in your family, and from your childcare provider.

To make pumping more successful, think ahead about how many times a day you will need to pump while away from your baby. The number of pumping sessions plus the number of feedings you and your baby have while you are at home equal the total number for that twenty-four hour period. If you think of the number of times you need to pump and nurse, rather than how often you need to pump at work, you may feel less stressed if you miss a pumping at work. Just don't make a regular habit of missing them.

You also need to have the person taking care of your baby on the same page as you. Ask your child care provider not to feed your baby an hour before pick him up. This way he'll be hungry and ready to nurse when you get home. Or if he can't wait that long, nurse him at the daycare before the ride home. To ensure he gets a good meal as soon as he sees you, don't pump at least an hour before you meet your baby so your breasts aren't too empty. I say empty, though your breasts are never really empty. There is always some milk in them.

Products

What products do you really need to breastfeed? All you need are your breasts and your baby, right? Right! But in this modern world, there are a few things to make it all a little easier or more comfortable.

Pumps
Pumps can be manual, battery operated, or electric. If you are going to be pumping a lot (ie: going back to work or school) an electric pump is better. If you are hesitant to buy an electric pump due to the cost, consider the large amount of money you spend an investment in your baby's health. I have seen many parents pay for a battery operated pump because it was cheaper, only to be disappointed by it's lack of power. Ask anyone you know who is pumping what they have found useful.

Make sure the pump you buy is a double pump. This means that it will pump milk from both of your breasts at the same time. This saves you time and increases your hormone levels so you produce more milk.

Manual pumps are powered by you. You squeeze the handle, which creates a suction and expresses milk. These can be great to use if you don't need to pump often or if you just need to express a little milk to soften engorged breasts.

Nursing Pads

Nursing pads are worn inside your bra to keep leaking milk from wetting your clothes. This can be a bit awkward during a work meeting! It's best to use disposable or cotton pads and change them often to avoid irritation and infection. You can also stop the leaking by applying pressure on your nipple for a few seconds. This really does work as long as your milk hasn't already made a big wet circle on your shirt. I was lucky that I wore a lab coat at work. There were a few times I forgot to wear nursing pads, and the lab coat concealed my mistake.

Nursing Bras

Nursing bras are made specifically for breastfeeding. The cup of the bra is attached to the strap by a small hook. Just unhook, lower the flap and your breast is exposed making it easier to breastfeed. It's best to wait until your milk has come in before you buy a nursing bra because your breasts will get bigger when this happens. If you do buy one before your milk has come in, make sure you can slip your hand into the cup while you have it adjusted to your size. This will allow more room for your breasts to fill once milk has come in.

If available in your area, I recommend having a trained sales person fit you for your bra. Most of us wear bras that are not really the right size. When you are nursing, a tight fitting bra can be uncomfortable and cause plugged milk ducts. If there is a postpartum clinic in a hospital in your area, ask if they will fit you for a bra. Some department stores have trained sales people too.

Nursing Aprons

These are the fashionable version of a blanket thrown over your breast and your baby. It is a piece of cloth that looks like a small poncho and comes in lovely fabrics and colors. It is a little nicer than the blanket idea, because you don't have to hold it in place. Since it goes over your neck and doesn't lie against your body, you can see your baby *and* the latch better. Personally, I never used a blanket or anything like this to cover myslef and my baby. I couldn't see what I was doing and always felt that my baby wasn't getting fresh air under there. It made nursing more awkward for me rather than less. So I learned to nurse in public without showing much and without caring who got an accidental peak. I also felt that my baby covered my breast so that I wasn't in danger of exposing myself. I have many tops that I wear in the summer that show more skin than I do while nursing. However, if a cover up makes you feel more comfortable nursing in public, I encourage you to use one. It's better to nurse in public covered up than not to nurse at all!

Nursing Tops

Nursing tops can also make breastfeeding in public easier. These are shirts that are specifically made for nursing. They have a second layer of material under the top layer. This second layer has an opening over your breast so that you only have to lift the top layer to expose your breasts. The second layer stays in place and covers your middle. You don't have to expose your stomach or back while breastfeeding.

Visualize It!

You have been away from your baby all day. Maybe you were at work or school, maybe you took a day for yourself. You pumped while away and find that pumping isn't as hard or burdensome as you thought it would be. Your body responds well to the pump and you feel grateful that you can be away from your baby and still give her your milk.

Now that you are back with your baby, you immediately feel an urge to nurse. Not just physically, because your breasts ache from their fullness, but emotionally, you want to be close to your baby and reconnect. Even though you miss your baby while you are away, you also appreciate the time you have together more after you have been gone. Your baby smells sweeter to you. Her eyes sparkle more brightly. She is just as excited to have Mama back too!

You settle into the rocking chair, take off your shoes, and bring your pillows around you. You kiss and coo over your baby. She plays a long for a bit, but is ready to nurse, so you latch her onto your breast. She is hungry! She nurses very excitedly at first, but once your milk lets down, she begins to relax and get into a rhythm. It feels good to have her nurse to empty your breasts and to take a break from the pump. You talk to her about your day and ask about hers. She seems to know what you are saying. She nurses a little longer than usual, just because she enjoys being close to you. Soon, she falls asleep and you rock with her awhile, enjoying this time together.

Debi's Thoughts

All three of my kids had problems with breastfeeding, but this was something I really wanted to do. I wanted to do it because of the health benefits. My mom breastfed 7 kids, so to me, this was just something you do.

Because I worked full time, this was my connection with my kids even if I wasn't with them. I would go away to work, and come back and be connected with them. As a full time worker, breastfeeding made me still feel like I was a mommy. If I gave formula, I would have felt like I could be easily replaced. I also had a stressful job, and breastfeeding gave me 15 minutes of just me and my baby. The more kids you have the more valuable that time is.

For me, pumping was easy, but it was challenging to find a place to pump. I worked at three different jobs with each kid and I always felt comfortable pumping at work. I never had a problem with my boss. People make it seem harder than it is. It was my 15 minutes to relax and think of my baby. I didn't need to sneak off to do it. I was going away from work for a purpose. I think there is a lot of misinformation out there about pumping. I talk to a lot of moms and they don't have the right kind of pump.

With my first kid, I was so uneducated about the whole breastfeeding thing. I wondered, "Why would anyone take a breastfeeding class?" When I had problems, finding resources was hard. I found answers in books. I just thought it had to get better. Between the second and the third kid, I found Jack Newman's book. It made me think that there was no problem I couldn't overcome. If you seek them out, there are resources!

Once I breastfed my kids, I realized that people really have to be committed to doing it. I would never have thought to congratulate a woman who was breastfeeding. Now I do because there are so many outside messages that are anti-breastfeeding.

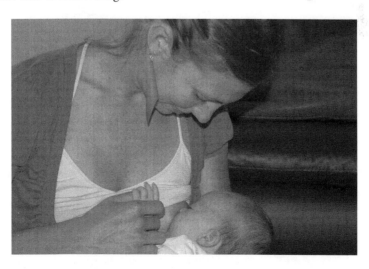

Chapter 11
Feel the Confidence

• • • • • • • • • • •

Breastfeeding my baby is pure pleasure.

I HOPE YOU ARE feeling a sense of confidence around the idea of breastfeeding. It is how your baby is supposed to be fed and it is what your breasts are meant to do. Surrounding yourself with supportive people and giving yourself time to learn how to breastfeed and to get to know your baby are the key ingredients for success. The visualization exercises will only add to that success.

I encourage you to do the visualization exercises written throughout the book and below while you are still pregnant to start creating your positive attitude about successful breastfeeding. By the time your baby is born, you will have no doubts that your body can produce the milk your baby needs! Read the affirmations in Appendix 1, or feel free to write your own.

If you are reading this after your baby is born, you will still benefit from the visualization exercises. We can change our way of thinking at any point in our journey if we find that we are creating obstacles for ourselves.

I wish you a wonderfully satisfying birth experience and a fabulously successful breastfeeding relationship! This is such a unique time in a person's life, in a family's life. With support and dedication, you can have a successful breastfeeding experience. Enjoy every moment and take lots of photos!

Read through the visualization exercise below all the way first. Allow yourself to be alone, in a quiet room, without interruption (unless you have someone read this aloud to you.) Once you feel comfortable with the imagery, close your eyes, and take a few deep breathes. Take a survey of your muscles. Relax those that are tense, starting with your face muscles, and work your way down to your toes. Once you feel that any tension has melted away, begin the exercise. If any negative thoughts enter your head, simply open your eyes, redirect your thoughts, and begin again. Enjoy the peace and allow the scenes of you and your baby together to play out.

Visualize it!

Now it is time to relax. Get into a comfortable position and close your eyes. Take a deep breathe in. Feel your breath move through your body down to your toes. Now exhale. Continue to breathe slowly and deeply, allowing the air to cleanse every part of your body.

Now focus on your eyes. Feel how effortlessly they close and how heavy your eyelids feel. The muscles around your eyes relax. Next the muscles on your forehead and around your mouth loosen. Your jaw is so relaxed, your lips and mouth may open a bit. Place your tongue behind your teeth and let it relax there comfortably. Let your mind release all thoughts. You are feeling very relaxed.

Feel your breath relax the muscles in your neck and shoulders. It's as though any tension in this area of your body is melting away. With each inhale you breathe in peace and calmness, while you exhale tension and stress. Breathe in peace and calmness. Exhale tension and stress. Your breathe moves into your arms and hands. These body parts feel very heavy as they relax. Your fingers may even tingle as the tension begins to leave them. All of the nerves in your body may tingle as they relax and you go deeper into relaxation.

Inhale deeply. Feel your breath move down to your chest and abdomen, bringing a sense of relaxation to these areas of your body. Your chest fills with a sense of wellbeing, and your abdomen softens as you go deeper into a state of relaxation. The nerves and cells of your breasts relax too. As your breasts relax, they are able to function more efficiently in producing milk for your baby. You start to feel a calmness come over you. Any noise that you hear only allows you to go deeper into a state of relaxation. Now move your breath into your pelvis. Feel the muscles in this area relax as the tension melts away. You are bringing positive energy to this area, which is such an important part of your body.

Now move the breath down to your legs and feet. Allow them to relax as you fill them with your breath. Again, all of the nerves and muscles in your legs and feet relax, as you melt away the tension. Your whole body feels heavy and limp as you enter an even deeper state of relaxation.

Now put your focus again on your breasts. They may tingle or feel heavy as they relax. Imagine the milk ducts inside your breasts. Now that they are relaxed, they do their job smoothly. When you are so relaxed, your body is able to function better. Milk production is effortless. Your body has the ancient wisdom needed to nourish your baby completely and totally. In this state of deep relaxation, you feel more and more confident that you are able to breastfeed your baby for as long as you want. You know that your body is doing just what it needs to do.

Inhale deeply and slowly. In your mind's eye, see your baby next to you as she starts to stir and wake up. She starts to stretch her body like a cat, waking from a long nap. You unswaddle her blankets, giving her more room to move. As you pick her up, you bring her to your face so you can kiss her cheek and smell her. Her breathe smells sweet, like your milk. Now hold your baby in your arms, as you prepare to nurse. You are comfortable because you have lots of pillows supporting your body and you are very relaxed. You are sinking into these pillows. See your baby in your arms. Feel the weight of your baby and how confident you are holding her. Her eyes are open now and she looks right at you. She knows you are her mother and that you are the one to give her nourishment. She looks to you for comfort and trusts you completely. This makes you feel more confident as a mother. Inhale deeply and slowly. Feel how wonderful it is to have your baby this close to you. Feel the fullness of your breasts telling you they are ready to be emptied by your baby.

You bring your baby into position so that you can feed her. This is getting easier and easier every time you do it. You and your baby are starting to get the hang of it! One of your hands is supporting your baby's head, while your other hand is supporting your breast. It feels so good to have your baby's body wrapped around yours. It feels as though you two have become one. You tickle your baby's lips with your nipple, coaxing her to open wide. It doesn't take much coaxing, though, as she is ready for your milk. As she opens her mouth wide, you bring her to your breast and she begins to suckle. It feels wonderful!

Inhale deeply and slowly. You go even deeper into a state of relaxation. Your baby continues to suckle milk from your breasts. She seems content and nurses in a rhythmic pattern, letting you know that she is getting milk. Her hand rises and rests comfortably on your breast, as though she is holding on to her favorite thing in the world. She looks up at you. The two of you make eye contact and a knowing moment passes. You know this is the way it should be. Your body was made to breastfeed your baby, and she knows that this is all the food she wants. It is the perfect connection for you and your baby, and it lays down the foundation for your relationship as she continues to grow and need you.

You have lost track of time. You feel so relaxed and contented while nursing your baby. She appears to be very contented as well. When she is done, she takes herself off of your breast and lets out a sigh. Again, you smell the sweetness of her breath.

Now it is time to end this session.

As I count to 5, you will begin to feel more alert. 1...2...feel the energy come back to your body, allowing your muscles to engage again. 3...start to move your arms and fingers. 4...begin to move your legs and toes. 5...open your eyes and feel refreshed and more confident than ever that you and your baby will have a successful breastfeeding relationship!

Chapter 12
For Those Unable To Breastfeed

....

I forgive my body and see all of its beauty.

THERE ARE TIMES WHEN a mother can't breastfeed her babies for whatever reason. If you have seen a lactation consultant or your health care provider, if you have pumped and taken galactogogues, if you have put most of your parenting effort into nursing, you can be confident that you have really tried everything. Are you seeing your effort rewarded by more milk supply, a better latch, or more weight gain? If not, you may have to decide to either offer breast milk with formula supplements or not offer breast milk at all. Not being able to breastfeed your baby can be very difficult to accept, especially if there has been a great deal of effort put into trying.

I know this can be a heartbreaking realization. I also know how hard it can be sometimes to persevere when there is no improvement. I expect moms to stay committed to the idea of breastfeeding their babies. I expect moms to try everything before giving up. I do not expect moms to work so hard at it that they resent the idea of breastfeeding and no longer enjoy time with their babies. Please stop before you get to this point! If you are unable to breastfeed your baby, it is ok to grieve this. Many of us imagine what nursing our babies will feel like before they are even born, especially if you have been doing the visualization exercises. It is sad and frustrating and disappointing when we can't live out these images. Grieving the loss of your image of breastfeeding is normal, and can be healthy and freeing.

Sometimes, there are ways to continue to give your baby breast milk, even if not exclusively. A mother may find that she does produce milk, it just isn't enough for her baby. She may choose to breastfeed and supplement with a bottle of formula after each feeding. Or she may choose to only nurse her baby for comfort, rather than nutrition. For example, she may nurse at night, or when she gets home from work, or whenever she and her baby are having a special moment. While this type of nursing pattern isn't enough for your baby's nutritional needs, it can satisfy the emotional needs of mom and baby. Never underestimate the value of fulfilling emotional needs.

I met a mother when her baby was about 4 weeks old. For financial reasons, she returned to work when her daughter was only 7 days old! She told me that she and her daughter were having a hard time getting the whole nursing thing down. Well, no wonder! She never had a chance to establish a good milk supply and her daughter never had a chance to learn to breastfeed. She was a teacher in a preschool and didn't have regular breaks to pump, so her supply was not what her baby needed it to be. She desperately wanted to nurse her baby and would put her to her breast as soon as she got home from work and on the weekends. However, it wasn't enough, so she supplemented with formula.

I watched this mother nurse her baby in my office. She was very stressed and her baby also appeared tense. I got the feeling that this mother was trying so hard because she had a true desire to give her baby optimal nutrition, but also because she felt she had no other choice if she was to be a good mother. Gently, I told her that she would not get her milk supply up to the level it needed to be to nourish her baby completely with the nursing and pumping pattern she had. After a very long discussion about the reality of the situation, she decided to nurse her baby when she got home if it seemed mutually desired. If nursing her baby felt like more stress than pleasure, she would discontinue nursing, and focus on snuggling with her baby, lying in bed with her, singing to her, etc. Her focus shifted from forcing breastfeeding to work to enjoying quality time with her daughter. Though she made a great effort, this mom was behind the eight ball. The time came for her to let go of her preconceived ideas and accept her reality and enjoy being a mom.

I know this example is an extreme one. But I wanted to illustrate how we can forget to enjoy our babies because we are too stressed out. If you have truly tried everything and are unable to nurse your baby, you can still consider yourself a good mom. You can still bond with your baby and shower him or her with love. Your baby can still grow to be a smart, successful person in life. You can let go of the guilt of not nursing your baby. You may not have the breastfeeding experience you desired, but you can be satisfied and proud of your efforts.

Below is an affirmation for those who are unable to nurse their babies, and are working through those feelings. Read the visualization exercise through first. Then find a quiet place to relax. If any negative thoughts creep into your head while you are doing the exercise, simply open your eyes and begin again. Redirect your thoughts toward more positive images. My hope is that by giving your subconscious positive messages you will find peace with the situation.

Visualize it!

Now it is time to relax. Get into a comfortable position and close your eyes. Take a deep breathe in. Feel your breath move through your body down to your toes. Now exhale. Continue to breathe slowly and deeply, allowing the air to cleanse every part of your body.

Now focus on your eyes. Feel how effortlessly they close and how heavy your eyelids feel. The muscles around your eyes relax. Next the muscles on your forehead and around your mouth loosen. Your jaw is so relaxed, your lips and mouth may open a bit. Place your tongue behind your teeth and let it relax there comfortably. Let your mind release all thoughts. You are feeling very relaxed.

Feel your breath relax the muscles in your neck and shoulders. It's as though any tension in this area of your body is melting away. With each inhale you breathe in peace and calmness, while you exhale tension and stress. Breathe in peace and calmness. Exhale tension and stress. Your breathe moves into your arms and hands. These body parts feel very heavy as they relax. Your fingers may even tingle as the tension begins to leave them. All of the nerves in your body may tingle as they relax and you go deeper into relaxation.

Inhale deeply. Feel your breath move down to your chest and abdomen, bringing a sense of relaxation to these areas of your body. Your chest fills with a sense of wellbeing, and your abdomen softens as you go deeper into a state of relaxation. The nerves and cells of your breasts relax too. As your breasts relax, they are able to function more efficiently in producing milk for your baby. You start to feel a calmness come over you. Any noise that you hear only allows you to go deeper into a state of relaxation. Now move your breath into your pelvis. Feel the muscles in this area relax as the tension melts away. You are bringing positive energy to this area, which is such an important part of your body.

Now move the breath down to your legs and feet. Allow them to relax as you fill them with your breath. Again, all of the nerves and muscles in your legs and feet relax, as you melt away the tension. Your whole body feels heavy and limp as you enter an even deeper state of relaxation.

With your eyes still closed, see yourself with your baby. You two are in your favorite place. This could be your bed, in a rocking chair, or outside in a place of nature. You are totally focused on your baby and she is totally focused on you. Your baby feels so warm in your arms and her body seems to almost "fit" in yours. Your start to hum to her and she looks up with alert eyes. She has heard you sing this song to her so many times before. She only knows it as "Mommy's Song".

While you hum softly to her, she finds your hand and wraps her fingers around your index finger. She has quite a grip! She is still focused on you with big, alert eyes and makes an "O" shape with her mouth, as though she is trying to sing along.

She wiggles her body a bit, finding a more comfortable spot next to you. You lift your finger to trace her cheek down to her chin. Her skin is so soft. You breathe her smell, your favorite smell in the world now. She is getting so chubby, growing before your eyes. There is still some sadness over the fact that you aren't nursing her, but you feel satisfied that you tried everything you could. You are grateful for these moments alone with your baby. You *are* bonding with her. She is getting to know her mommy and how much her mommy loves her.

Now focus your attention onto your body. The flaws you saw before are gone and now you see how beautiful your body is. Your baby fits perfectly in your body; you two are one when you hold her. You forgive your body for not producing the milk your baby needed. You feel peace over it. You feel comfortable in your body.

Now it is time to end the session. When you are ready, slowly wiggle your toes, then your fingers. Start to wake your body again. Take a deep breath in and open your eyes.

Appendix I
Affirmations for Successful Breastfeeding

• • • • • • • • • • • •

I feel my breasts increasing in size, preparing for the production of milk.

My breasts know exactly how much milk my baby needs.

My breasts flow with an abundance of wonderful milk for my baby.

My baby gains weight feeding only from my breasts.

The colostrum I produce in the beginning is liquid gold for my baby.

My milk comes in very quickly.

My milk offers my baby all of the nutrition she needs to grow up healthy and strong.

It feels good to have my baby in my arms suckling from my breasts.

As my baby grows and his nutritional needs change, my breasts also change the quality of my milk so that my baby gets exactly what he needs.

My baby is satisfied at my breast. She coos and falls asleep after each meal.

My milk is laying down the foundation for optimal health for my baby.

I know that my milk will make my baby smarter today and in her future.

I am committed to giving my baby milk from my breasts.

I enjoy breastfeeding. It allows me to be close to my baby.

Breastfeeding allows me the convenience of feeding my baby whenever and wherever she needs it.

My breasts feel full of milk before each feeding and empty afterwards.

I love to feel the tingling sensation of the "let down reflex". It tells me that my body is ready for my baby to nurse.

I feel confident nursing my baby in public.

I am supported by my family and by society to nurse my baby because it is the best thing for her.

I effortlessly latch my baby onto my breast.

I feel relaxed when my baby is nursing.

My milk is rich and abundant.

I know how to breastfeed my baby. It is part of the ancient animal instinct that has allowed women to nourish their babies for centuries.

Nursing my baby is what my breasts are intended to do.

My breasts are beautiful, with a beautiful purpose.

I read my baby's hunger cues and offer him my breast without any fuss.

My favorite moment is snuggling with my baby while she is latched onto my breast.

My partner is committed to giving our baby breast milk.

I trust my body to nourish my baby.

I am grateful for my body's wisdom in feeding my baby.

I love my body.

I am impressed by my body's effortless production of milk for my baby.

My body knows how to nourish my baby.

My baby wants the milk my body produces.

My baby is healthy.

Breastfeeding my baby is pure pleasure.

I successfully breastfeed my baby into childhood.

My baby wants the milk I have to offer.

I have patience.

Breastfeeding my baby gets easier and easier every time I do it.

Breastfeeding feels wonderful.

I love to nurse my baby!

I am grateful that my body knows how to nourish my baby.

My body looks beautiful.

Appendix 2
Writing A Birth Plan

• • • • • • • • • • •

Here are some things to discuss with your partner and possibly include in your birth plan.

Labor & Delivery

Who will be in the room while you are laboring? Who will be there while you give birth?

Do you want to wear your own clothes?

Which of the following techniques help you feel relaxed?
    Soft music
    Low lighting
    Pleasant fragrances
    Massage
    Light touch
    Talking to someone
    Taking a bath or shower
    Taking a walk
    Acupressure
    Changing positions
    Heat
    Cold

How do you like information presented to you? Do you like to be given many choices or do you prefer to have someone recommend what you should do?

How mobile do you want to be during labor? Free to move around? Free to move in bed? Not important to you?

What would you like to eat and drink while in labor?

Of course, you want to avoid medical interventions unless necessary for the safety of you and your baby. Rate the following interventions on how much you want to avoid them. Rate them from 15 (1 means you don't mind the intervention, 5 means you want to avoid it at all costs)

Induction before or after your due date
Pitocin
Rupture of your membranes (breaking your bag of waters)
Cesarean section
Pain medication
Internal fetal scalp monitor
Continuous fetal monitoring
Having an IV
Episiotomy
Having baby separated from mom

Do you want to be offered pain medication, or given pain medication only if you ask for it?

What labor positions would you like to try?
Semi-inclined in bed
In bathtub or shower
On a birthing ball
Squatting
On hands and knees
Side lying in bed
Standing/Leaning against someone or something
Other

How would you like to push your baby? Do you want coached pushing (someone telling you when to push)? Spontaneous bearing down (you only push when your body tells you to)? Do you want to squat or use a birth bar while you push?

Do you want photos or video taken of the labor, birth, or postpartum period?

BREASTFEEDING

When do you want to start nursing your baby?

How do you feel about pacifiers?

How do you feel about giving your baby bottles and/or formula?

Do you want your baby to stay in your room with you, or will you want your baby to spend some time in the baby nursery with the nurses?

Does your birth place have a lactation consultant or someone on staff to assist with breastfeeding? Do you want them to visit you while you are there?

POSTPARTUM & BABY CARE

Do you want to see your placenta?

Do you want the umbilical cord to be cut immediately after delivery or do you want that delayed? Do you want your partner to cut the cord?

Do you want eye care to be done immediately after delivery or to be delayed?

Do you want the baby's bath to be delayed until after initial bonding with you? Do you want you or your partner to give the first bath?

Do you plan to circumcise your son?

OTHER THINGS TO THINK ABOUT

If you are having a home or birth center birth, what are your plans in case of transferring to the hospital?

If you have a cesarean section, who do you want present? In how much detail do you want things explained to you? When do you want to see/touch your baby? When do you want to breastfeed?

If your baby is separated from you for medical reasons, do you want someone you know with the baby at all times? Who? Do you want to pump your milk?

It is important to have good, open communication with your partner, doula, and health care provider so that you can have a satisfying birth experience. There is also a fine line between making sure you get what you want and respecting your provider's medical opinion if things stray from normal. It's important to have conversations about how information will be presented to you if complications arise *before* you go into labor. It's a good idea to write your birth plan with your partner so you both have your wishes known. Then review it with your provider and your doula. Take a copy to your birth place so everyone there will know your plan too.

Appendix 3
Galactogogues

• • • • • • • • • • •

Galactogogues are medications or herbs that can increase a woman's milk supply. They do not replace the baby suckling or pumping to increase supply, rather they can help give that extra boost. They are also not a first line of attack. If you find that your supply is down, see your health care provider first. Once a medical reason for a decreased milk supply has been ruled out, and it is determined that increased breastfeeding and pumping are not enough, ask about using galactogogues.

Pharmaceutical Galactogogues

The following drugs are prescribed for stimulating milk production as an "off-label" use. This means that the drugs are designated by the Food and Drug Administration (FDA) for other uses, but because they happen to also benefit milk production, they are prescribed for that reason without the FDA's designation as a galactogogues. This is a legal and common practice among health care providers.

Metoclopramide (brand name: Reglan)

Metoclopramide is the most common drug prescribed to increase breast milk production. It is an antiemetic and used to treat reflux in infants. Common side effects for the mother using metoclopramide are restlessness, drowsiness, fatigue, and diarrhea. Some women have experienced confusion, dizziness, depression and anxiety when using this drug. If this is the case, the drug should be discontinued.

Domperidone (brand name: Motilium)

Domperidome is a dopamine antagonist, which increases prolactin levels. It has fewer side effects than metoclopramide, which makes it more appealing to use, though women may experience dry mouth, headache and abdominal cramping. It is not readily available in the United States because of a warning issued by the FDA based in safety concerns with IV drug use and risks associated with drug importation, despite the fact that it has been used all over the world for years, and has an excellent safety record. (12) Because domperidone has not been through the FDA process and has some controversy surrounding it, it can be difficult to find a doctor willing to prescribe it and a pharmacy able to provide it.

Herbal Galactogogues

Herbs have been used throughout time all and over the world to stimulate milk production. There are some studies to support their use, however, herbs are no longer evaluated by the FDA. Therefore, there is no standard dosing or preparation, so there may be some risk in taking them.

Fenugreek
Fenugreek is a spice used in Indian and Middle Eastern dishes. It is also the most commonly used herbal galactogogue in North America. The usual dose is one to four capsules taken three to four times a day, though there is no standard dosing. (12) It can also be taken as a tincture or a tea, though it is difficult to get enough of the herb in tea form. You should see a difference in milk supply within 3 days. If not, fenurgreek may not affect your milk supply afterall. Side affects are rare, but include a maple syrup ordor to your sweat and urine, diarrhea, and increased asthmatic symptoms. (12)

Blessed Thistle
Blessed thistle is often taken with fenugreek. It can be found in the form of capsule, tea, and tincture (the last two forms can be quite bitter). Usual dosing is 3 capsules 3 times a day, or 20 drops of the tincture 3 times a day. (13)

Milk Thistle
Not to be confused with blessed thistle, milk thistle has been used for centuries. To take as a tea, simmer one teaspoon of crushed seeds in an eight ounce cup of water for ten minutes. (12)

Other Herbs
- Alfalfa
- Spirulina

- Goat's Rue
- Raspberry Leaf
- Fennel
- Brewer's Yeast
- Stinging Nettle
- Dill Seed
- Oatmeal (not an herb, but may help milk production if eaten daily)

Resources

Here are some of my favorite websites that provide great information for breastfeeding moms.

The International Lactation Consultant Association
The International Lactation Consultant Association is a good source for finding a lactation consultant in your area. These lactation consultants have worked with breastfeeding moms and babies for many hours and passed a certifying exam before becoming Internationally Board Certified Lactation Consultants (IBCLCs).
http://www.ilca.org/falc.html

Le Leche League (LLL)
Le Leche League is an organization that was started by a few moms who got together back in the 1960s to help each other with their breastfeeding issues. It is now an international organization. Free meetings are offered all over the country. Go to the website to find a meeting near you.
http://www.llli.org/WebUS.html

Dr. Jack Newman
Dr. Jack Newman and Edith Kernerman are experts in the field of breastfeeding. Their website offers video clips, education, and the chance to ask them your questions.
http://www.drjacknewman.com/

Kelly Mom
This website offers evidence based information on breastfeeding and parenting.
http://kellymom.com/

Breastfeeding.Com

Video clips, educational tools, and fun tidbits make this website a good place to turn for information.

http://www.breastfeeding.com/

DoulaMatch.net

DoulaMatch.net is a doula referral database for finding available, trained and certified doulas. Families, health care providers and referral coordinators search for available doulas based on due date and zip code; and, can review certifications, experience, services and fees to find the doula that perfectly matches their criteria.

www.doulamatch.net

HypnoBirthing: http://www.hypnobirthing.com/
HypnoBabies: http://www.hypnobabies.com/

The websites above can help you find a hypnobirthing or hypnobabies class in your area.

Baby Friendly Hospitals

To find an updated list of Baby Friendly hospitals, go to http://www.babyfriendlyusa.org/eng/03.html.

I would love to hear from you! Please email me about your experience with the affirmations and visualizations or any questions you might have. You can contact me through my website at www.kristinacnm.com.

Bibliography

1. **Gartner, L.M., et al.** Breastfeeding and the Use of Human Milk. *American Academy of Pediatrics.* [Online] Feb 2005. [Cited: August 2, 2010.] http://aappolicy.aappublications.org/cgi/content/full/pediatrics;115/2/496.

2. Breastfeeding Among US Children Born 1999-2007, CDC National Immunization Survey. *Center for Disease Control and Prevention.* [Online] July 27, 2010. [Cited: August 2, 2010.] http://www.cdc.gov/breastfeeding/data/NIS_data/.

3. **Walker, M.** *Core Curriculum for Lactation Consultant Practice.* Sudbury : Jones and Bartlett Publishers, 2002. 0-7637-1038-5.

4. **Biancuzzo, M.** *Breastfeeding the Newborn, Clinical Strategies for Nurses.* St.Louis : Mosby, 1999. 0-8151-2453-8.

5. The Ten Steps to Successful Breastfeeding. *Baby-Freindly USA, Inc.* [Online] 2010. [Cited: August 2, 2010.] http://www.babyfriendlyusa.org/eng/10steps.html.

6. Research Shows Doulas Make a Difference. *DONA International.* [Online] 2005. [Cited: August 2, 2010.] http://www.dona.org/resources/research.php.

7. What is Colostrum? How Does it Benefit My Baby? *http://www.llli.org/FAQ/colostrum.html.* [Online] Le Leche League International, October 13, 2006. [Cited: August 2, 2010.] http://www.llli.org/FAQ/colostrum.html.

8. *Kangaroo care and breastfeeding of mother-preterm infant dyad 0-18 months: a randomized, controlled trial.* **Hake-Brooks, SJ and Anderson, GC.** 2008, Neonatal Network, pp. 151-9.

9. *A randomized, controlled trial of kangaroo mother care: results of follow up at one year of corrected age.* **Charpak, N, et al.** 2001, Pediatrics, pp. 1072-9.

10. *Breastfeeding and contraception.* **Too, Sooi-Ken.** 2003, British Journal of Midwifery, pp. 88-93.

11. Proper Handling and Storage of Human Milk. *Center for Disease Control and Prevention.* [Online] March 4, 2010. [Cited: July 1, 2010.] http://www.cdc.gov/breastfeeding/recommendations/handling_breastmilk.htm.

12. Newman, J. and Kernerman, E. Herbal Remedies for Milk Supply. Newman Breastfeeding Clinic and Institute. [Online] 2009. [Cited May 23, 2010.] http://www.drjacknewman.com/help/Herbal%Remedies%20 for%20Milk%20Supply.asp.

13. Montgomery, A. and Wright, N. Protocol #9: Use of galactogues in intiating or augmenting maternal milk supply. ABM Protocols. [Online] The Academy of Breastfeeding Medicine, July 30, 2004. [Cited: May 23, 2010.] http://www.bfmed.org/Resources/Protocols.aspx

About the Author

Kristina Chamberlain is a Certified Nurse-Midwife and International Board Certified Lactation Consultant. She has worked with women and their families for over 15 years as a doula, educator, nurse, and midwife. She graduated from the midwifery program at the University of Washington, and continued to complete a post-master's program in women's health. Currently, she has a clinical practice and also teaches childbirth and breastfeeding classes. Through her work, she believes she is saving the world 1 birth and 2 breasts at a time!

She lives in Bellevue, WA with her wonderful husband and two fabulous daughters.

Manufactured By: RR Donnelley
                    Momence, IL USA
                    September, 2010